ROCK ART
of the
LOWER PECOS

ROCK ART
of the
LOWER PECOS

CAROLYN E. BOYD

TEXAS A&M UNIVERSITY PRESS
COLLEGE STATION

To my mom and dad for igniting my curiosity
and to my husband for fanning the flame.

Copyright © 2003 by Carolyn E. Boyd
Manufactured in the United States of America
All rights reserved
First edition

The paper used in this book meets the minimum
requirements of the American National Standard for
Permanence of Paper for Printed Library Materials,
z39.48-1984.
Binding materials have been chosen for durability.
⊗

Library of Congress Cataloging-in-Publication Data

Boyd, Carolyn E., 1958–
      Rock art of the lower Pecos / Carolyn E. Boyd.—1st ed.
         p. cm.—(Texas A&M University anthropology series ; no. 8)
Includes bibliographical references and index.
      ISBN 1-58544-259-3 (cloth : alk. paper)
      1. Indians of North America—New Mexico—Antiquities.
2. Indians of North America—Pecos River Valley (N.M. and Tex.)—
Antiquities. 3. Petroglyphs—Pecos River Valley (N.M. and Tex.)
4. Rock paintings—Pecos River Valley (N.M. and Tex.)
5. Pecos River Valley (N.M. and Tex.)—Antiquities. I. Title.
   II. Texas A&M University anthropology series ; no. 8.
      E78.N65 B69 2003
      759.01'13'09764—dc21
                                      2003003570

All illustrations are by the author, unless otherwise noted.

Contents

Illustrations

Acknowledgments

**But they that wait upon the Lord shall renew their strength;
they shall mount up with wings as eagles . . .**

ISAIAH 40:31

I want to express my deepest thanks to the many people who have helped me in the process of researching, writing, and illustrating this book. First, I thank my husband, best friend, and colleague, Phil Dering. His support throughout the production of this book was incalculable. He spent vast amounts of time with me in the field photographing the rock art in addition to reviewing chapters and making valuable contributions to the text. Second, I thank my children Noah, Jeff, and Audrey, for their patience and encouragement when I left to do field work or disappeared behind the computer or drawing board for days on end. I could not have accomplished this without them. I also thank my parents, Jody and Walker Boyd. They were a continuous source of encouragement and inspiration.

I am also indebted to friends and fellow scholars who contributed countless hours by my side, surveying the canyons of the lower Pecos and meticulously recording rock art. Damon Burden was an invaluable help in the collection of data for this book, as was Jessica Lee and Joan Baker. Jessica and Damon also assisted in the production of some of the rock art panel renderings.

I want to thank the land owners who were so gracious in allowing me access to their properties and who are such faithful stewards of the art and archaeology on their land. It is only because of their generosity and foresight that this book was possible. No words can express how grateful I am for the help, encouragement, and hospitality provided by Jack and Missy Harrington. I would also like to thank Darrell, Mary Jane, and Jim Hargrove, Jack and Wilmuth Skiles, Carol Hayman and Bob White, and all the other families that granted me access to their property to conduct research. The Seminole Canyon State Park personnel were also a reliable source of assistance. I thank them for this, for their friendship, and for their dedication to protecting the rock art of Seminole Canyon State Park. I am grateful to the National Park Service for the assistance provided in accessing rock art within their boundaries and for their efforts toward education and preservation. And I would especially like to thank the Rock Art Foundation for their tireless devotion to increasing awareness and understanding of this precious cultural heritage.

Thank you to Megan Biesele, Tom Hester, David Whitley, Chris Chippindale, David Lewis-Williams, Dee Ann Story, Harry Shafer,

Alston Thoms, Lee Cronk, Jeff Cohen, Kathy Dettwyler, Gentry Steele, Eunice Barkes and the many other colleagues who offered constructive comments and encouragement throughout the evolution of this book. Special thanks go to Robyn Lyle for her editing of the original manuscript and her technical assistance in its production.

And finally, thank you to the Texas Archeological Society Donor's Fund for the financial support that made the summer 1997 field season a possibility; and I offer a special thanks to the Texas Archeological Society Rock Art Recording Task Force volunteers for all they have done and continue to do to document Texas rock art. Their work will benefit researchers throughout the years ahead.

ROCK ART
of the
LOWER PECOS

One

THE WORK OF ART

Art is the expression and communication of man's deepest instincts and emotions
reconciled and integrated with his social experience and cultural heritage.
While the framework of laws, governments, and empires decays and disintegrates,
the social attitudes and values that the art of a people records . . .
remain vivid and eloquent for all time.

R. MURKERJEE, *The Social Function of Art*

Scholars, in particular art historians, have long recognized that the art of ancient societies serves as an enduring record of intellectual and spiritual expression, a unique source for deriving inferences about the past. Professional archaeologists have been reluctant to access this same information in prehistoric art. The prevailing attitude has been, and in many cases still is, that research directed toward the interpretation of art cannot be accorded scientific status and thus should not be the subject of archaeological study. Instead, archaeological research has focused more on the material aspects of life, avoiding the areas of human cognition or symbolic structures.

Perhaps this reluctance to develop the scientific methods necessary to study rock art stems from our Western conception or "abstraction" of art. In contemporary Western society, we tend to focus on the aesthetic, decorative, and recreational nature of art and either deemphasize, ignore, or deny the utility of art. Although archaeologists have been reticent to integrate art with archaeological data, rock art images decorate the covers of innumerable professional archaeological reports and texts. Rarely, however, do these documents include any discussion about rock art. The images are used merely as decoration, further perpetuating our Western impression of art as the embellishment of an object beyond its ostensible purpose. In non-Western societies, however, art objects are often considered essential and powerful instruments— not passive props but active participants in the sociocultural system within which they were produced.

This book presents a study of the prehistoric, hunter-gatherer rock art of the lower Pecos River region, in southwestern Texas and northern Mexico (fig. 1.1). Archaeological research in the lower Pecos River region has produced an unusually rich collection of material culture, yet many questions about the

FIG. I.I   Pecos River–style rock art from Panther Cave (41VV83), Seminole Canyon.
This illustration represents approximately 8 meters of the 40-meter panel depicted on
the shelter wall of Panther Cave. Redrawn from Kirkland and Newcomb (1967:63).

region's inhabitants remain unanswered. Researchers have either failed to recognize the contribution of rock art to the reconstruction of this prehistoric cultural system or recognized its value but lacked the empirical methods necessary to access the information provided in the art. As a result, the prehistoric rock art of the region represents a neglected data resource. I suggest that this data resource may relate to subjects as diverse as hunter-gatherer land use, subsistence, technology, social organization, worldview, cosmology, and ritual activity.

The primary objectives of this book are to (1) demonstrate that prehistoric art can be explained using scientific methods; (2) synthesize scientifically generated rock art interpretations to address issues regarding hunter-gatherer belief systems and lifeways of the lower Pecos Archaic; (3) establish that rock art production was a mechanism for social and environmental adaptation; and (4) show that not only the artist but also the art itself served

as an active agent in the social, economic, and ideological affairs of the community.

These objectives are addressed through the analysis of five rock art panels in the lower Pecos region—Rattlesnake Canyon, White Shaman, Panther Cave, Mystic Shelter, and Cedar Springs. During the course of the analysis, recurring themes, or "motifs," are identified in the art, and ethnological data are used to formulate hypotheses regarding three of these motifs. The hypotheses are subsequently tested against the lower Pecos material record and evaluated in relation to well-documented neuroscience research associated with altered states of consciousness. All resulting data are considered within the context of the social and biophysical environment of the region.

I argue that the art and artists of the lower Pecos were an integral part of hunter-gatherer adaptation in the region. More specifically, I contend that rock art production was part of an "adaptive strategy." Broadly defined, an adaptive strategy is "the set of culturally transmitted behaviors—extractive, exploitative, modifying, manipulative, competitive, mutualistic, and the like—with which a population interacts with its natural or social environment" (Kirch 1980:129). I suggest that the art was a vehicle through which intangible assets were shared, allowing individual knowledge to become group knowledge. Produced by an egalitarian society that likely viewed direct instruction as inappropriate and a threat to autonomy, rock art facilitated the "indirect" dissemination of information necessary for successful exploitation of the hunting and gathering niche—information regarding the biophysical environment, animal behavior, and ecological relationships. Additionally, the art and artists were active agents in creating, maintaining, reproducing, and challenging existing social relations and religious identities. The rock art performed *work*—it was a powerful form of technology used to ensure the continuation of self and society in the lower Pecos region four thousand years ago.

What Is This Thing Called "Art"?

Before we can comprehend how art *works,* we should consider what art *is.* Rudyard Kipling, in *Conundrum of the Workshop,* written in 1890, poetically framed the crucial question that continues to be asked: "When the flush of a new-born sun fell on Eden's green and gold, / Our father Adam sat under the tree and scratched with a stick in the mould; / And the first rude sketch that the world had seen was joy to his mighty heart, / Till the Devil whispered behind the leaves, "It's pretty. But is it Art?" What art is (and is not) has been debated for ages and will likely continue to be hotly contested. It is not my intention to enter into this debate by offering another definition for this elusive phenomenon; there are already as many definitions for the term as there are books on the subject. It is important, however,

to consider the influence Western definitions of fine art have on our perceptions of art from prehistory, such as the rock art of the lower Pecos River region.

ART FOR ART'S SAKE

Although the term "beaux arts" first appeared as a French phrase during the mid-seventeenth century, not until 1880 did the word "art" as it is currently used appear in an English dictionary (Kristeller 1970; Staniszewski 1995). During the second half of the nineteenth century, a powerful trend in aesthetic reflection claimed that art had no practical purpose at all. In fact, it did not aim at anything beyond the very contemplation of the work of art; thus was born the phrase "art for art's sake." The production of art was believed to be a leisure activity, a form of play; it was an enterprise to be engaged in only after attending to the necessary affairs of the day (Barasch 1998).

How do we, bound by the ideals of Western culture, define art today? Has it changed dramatically since the 1800s? According to art historian Mary Anne Staniszewski (1995:111), art is defined today as "an original creation produced by an individual gifted with genius . . . an object of aesthetic beauty, separate from everyday life. . . . [Art is] not solely political propaganda, not a religious nor sacred object, neither magic nor craft." If we accept this definition, the vast corpus of images we cherish today as works of art cannot be considered Art (a capital A refers to the contemporary Western definition of art). According to this definition, Art would be a relatively recent phenomenon, an invention of the modern era (Kristeller 1970; Staniszewski 1995). Not even the masterpieces produced during the height of the Renaissance—such as Michelangelo's *Creation of Adam* and da Vinci's *Last Supper*—can be considered Art. Perhaps the definition presented by Staniszewski does not reflect the popular perception of what art is or is not; I know it certainly does not reflect mine. Ask friends, however, to explain how they select artwork for their home or office and you will likely be answered, "it moves me," "it's really pretty," "it matches my sofa," "it was cheap," or "I didn't select it, the decorator did." It is highly unlikely that you will hear: "I don't especially like the way it looks, but it is very useful."

To gain insight into how the layperson defines art, students in my anthropology of art class at Texas A&M University conducted a survey of more than five hundred people. Individuals were asked to rank, in order of preference, definitions of art that are currently found in the literature. The results were revealing. More than 75 percent of the individuals surveyed selected a definition emphasizing the notion that art is created for the sole purpose of being aesthetically pleasing to people within society and with minimal purpose beyond that of intrinsic enjoyment. Works of art, according to the favored definition, are created by people primarily to be enjoyed or appreciated. Of the individuals surveyed, 15 percent selected a definition emphasizing human skill as the dominant criteria for art with no reference to aesthetics. Only 10 percent selected a definition that presents art as utilitarian, a part of a system of tools and techniques by means of which people relate to their physical and social environment. In Western societies, art is not viewed as utilitarian; rather, it is viewed as an object of aesthetic beauty produced by skilled individuals acting on their own free will.

ART FOR LIFE'S SAKE

In many non-Western societies art, as described above, is neither a linguistic category nor a social practice. Objects produced by individuals in non-Western societies, however, are removed from their cultural context and displayed in Western museums; they are appropriated and transformed into objects of art. A recent exhibit at the Yale University Art Gallery entitled *Baule: African Art/Western Eyes,* was described as being "many things all at once . . . a gathering of astonishingly beautiful objects; a radical rethinking of traditional museum presentations of art; and perhaps most important, a suggested model for a new kind of art history in which the very act of seeing is redefined" (Cotter 1997:39). Although Baule sculptures have been treasured as works of art in Western museums for most of the twentieth century, the Baule themselves have no single word for art (Vogel 1997). In "Beyond Beauty: Art That Takes Action," an article in the *New York Times* about the Baule exhibit, H. Cotter notes that the Baule "value the work they make far less for what it looks like than what for *what it can do,* socially and spiritually" (1997:39; emphasis added).

Among the Baule of Africa and countless other non-Western societies, art *works;* it *performs.* Among the Abelam of New Guinea, paintings that are ranked as the "best" by members in the community earn this ranking based on their effectiveness in ritual. This effectiveness does not go unnoticed by members of other communities. If one community appears to be producing a more bountiful yam harvest, the painting style of the more successful yam producers is adopted by neighboring communities in an effort to increase the effectiveness of their own paintings (Forge 1967). Forge (1967:83) stated that "the skillful artist who satisfies the aesthetic sense and produces beauty is rewarded not for the beauty itself but because the beauty, although not recognized as such, is regarded as power."

The same is true for Australian Aboriginal art. For example, Walbiri describe all designs as *wiri,* a term meaning strong, powerful, and important. Although these designs differ in relative importance and power, they are all considered to be efficacious; they are "valuable instruments" (Munn 1973:55). Aboriginal art, however, is now accepted in the institutional art world as "fine art." It is defined as fine art by its purchasers, such as galleries, collectors, and museums, not by the individuals who produced the objects. These works of "art" are then displayed with no mention of the object's original function, which is often religious and, to some degree, political in nature (Morphy 1991). As Maquet (1986:70) noted, "When artifacts are uprooted from their culture of origin and are assimilated in another, several phenomena of culture change are triggered. Usually there is a shift from one aesthetic locus to another, and a metamorphosis of an object from instrument to art."

Anthropologists who study the arts in non-Western societies usually acknowledge the utility of art (R. Anderson 1979; Forge 1967; Murkerjee 1971). Some researchers, however, suggest not only that there is utility in art but also that a general behavior of art has played a critical role in human biological adaptation (Cooke and Turner 1999; Dissanayake 1988, 1992). Ellen Dissanayake (1988, 1992) argued that a behavior of art, or "making special," is essential to human biological adaptation. She described the behavior of art as follows: "the manufacture or expression of what are commonly called 'the arts' is based on a universal inherited propensity in human nature to make some objects and activities special" (1988:107). Dissanayake presented a convincing and positive view of art as "life-sustaining," as "art for life's sake." She stated, "The fact that people everywhere value the arts and take the trouble to express themselves aesthetically suggests to an evolutionary biologist that there is a reason: doing this (rather than not doing this) contributes to human evolutionary fitness. Faced with the overwhelming evidence that people everywhere make and respond to the arts, the ethologist would have to presuppose that the arts must have survival value" (1988:62). Using an ethological perspective, Dissanayake argued that art is a universal and essential human behavior that is as characteristic of humankind as toolmaking, symbolization, language, and the development of culture.

Archaeologists have long been interested in the study of toolmaking behavior and the products of such behavior, readily accepting the utility of both the behavior and the product in human adaptation. Only recently, however, have studies of prehistoric art begun to recognize that art and artists are active agents in the negotiation of social relations and in the reproduction of society (Biesele 1983; Conkey 1984; Dowson 1998; Irwin 1994; Lewis-Williams 1995a; Whitley 1994a). Expressive forms, such as storytelling and rock paintings, are integral parts of a hunting and gathering adaptation. Individuals and social groups act through expressive forms to articulate meanings that must be shared in order to perpetuate society. These expressive forms, which include rock art, "perform work." They work to "indirectly" instruct and communicate information necessary to make certain adaptations successful within egalitarian societies where direct instruction generates an adverse reaction. In hunter-gatherer societies, the work performed by expressive forms may be unachievable through any other means. Biesele (1983:59) stated that among the hunting and gathering San of South Africa, "the wresting of a livelihood from a harsh environment with handmade tools, depending as absolutely as it has upon social cooperation of a very particular sort, has been intimately connected with the visual and verbal arts which 'make sense' and also provide a framework for survival information."

If art behavior is essential to human adaptation and the product of the behavior is an instrument in the reproduction of society, is it correct to refer to the behavior and the product as "art"? Contemporary Western definitions of art state that it is "separate from everyday life" and "nonutilitarian."

It's Pretty, but Is It Art?

The rock paintings that line canyon and shelter walls of the lower Pecos have been described as "beautiful," "magnificent," and even "pretty"—but are they Art? Rock paintings and engravings have been referred to in the literature for hundreds of years as "rock art," but again, are they Art? The rock art of the lower Pecos, as with prehistoric imagery around the world, is becoming increasingly admired for its looks, its aesthetic value. These images decorate homes, coffee mugs, clothing, stationery, even doormats—appropriated by our culture and transformed into Art.

By modern Western definition, the pictographic images of the lower Pecos are not Art nor are the vast majority of images from prehistory that are referred to as "rock art," "ceramic art," "body art," and so on. They are "power-full" instruments that serve to express functions in specific contexts and are the visual by-products of an essential human behavior— the behavior of art. Should we then cease to refer to this imagery as "rock art"? We could try to use a less value-laden term, perhaps rock imagery or rock paintings and engravings. But the use of these terms can also become problematic. Changing the term we use to refer to these images will not change the way they are perceived by archaeologists, art historians, anthropologists, or the general public. We cannot, after all, deny the aesthetic pleasure we derive when we view these masterpieces from prehistory. As members of a Western society, we can appreciate them aesthetically; however, we must try to explain them scientifically, recognizing their adaptive, utilitarian, and functional importance.

As I see it, the problem is not in the term "rock art," but in Western insecurities about what art *does.* Why should we change the term used to refer to this type of visual imagery just because it does not fit our only recently developed and extremely imperialistic definition of art? In ten years the "contemporary" definition of art will likely be different from what it is today. And what will we do then, change terms again? The solution is not to change the term but, through research and education, to broaden our understanding and appreciation for the "work" of art—past, present, and future.

In the following chapters, I seek to unveil the work of art and artist in the lower Pecos River region four thousand years ago, demonstrating the vital role served by both in the continuation of self and society. I begin by presenting an introduction to the region's environment, its people and their art. In chapter 3 I put forth a research design that seeks to integrate rock art with other archaeological data and subjects it to analogous methods of analysis. I also present the results of my analysis of five Pecos River–style rock art panels in which I identified three recurring motifs in the art. In chapter 4 I explain the first recurring motif as imagery associated with shamanic journeys to the otherworld and altered states of consciousness. In chapter 5 I identify the second and third recurring motifs as pictographic representations of peyote and datura, two powerful plants used as a sacrament, medicine, and bridge to the otherworld. In the final chapter, I argue that the work of art and artist was ingrained in the technological, social, and ideological concerns of the community and an integral part of hunter-gatherer adaptation in the lower Pecos River region during the Archaic period.

Two

ENVIRONMENT AND CULTURAL SETTING
OF THE LOWER PECOS RIVER REGION

The canyon by which we left the Pecos, bearing to the southeast, was rough and
difficult. Chaparral (here very thick), cactus, and various stony gullies made the march
for a few miles very severe. Reached elevated tables, at noon reached fine grass. . . .
We find the country to consist of a vast table elevation cut up by some great convulsion
of old time into numerous ravines or canyons. The valleys are rendered pretty
by groves of live oak and cedar, with occasional groups of other trees whose names I do not know.

WILLIAM H. C. WHITING, "Journal of William Henry Chase Whiting"

The lower Pecos is a rough, rocky, dry country. Early European travelers found the region forbidding if not impassable. In fact, the accounts often dwell on the extreme difficulties encountered when simply passing through the area. The diary of Gaspar Castaño de Sosa has two very telling entries. First, he notes that "they found the Rio Salado [Pecos River], . . . though they could not enter into it on account of the many sharp rocks *(pena tajada)* and ravines." While searching for a passable crossing for two weeks, the Spanish party began to despair of the rough country. "On the approach to the Pecos River, the partys *[sic]* used up in these mountains 25 dozen horseshoes, because it was not possible to travel by any other route" (Schroeder and Matson, 1965:41, 49).

Lower Pecos Environment

Centered near the confluence of the Pecos River with the Rio Grande, the northern half of the region lies in Texas and the southern half in Coahuila, Mexico (fig. 2.1). Much of the landscape is dominated by the canyons that incise the southwestern edge of the Edwards Plateau (Fenneman 1931). These deep and narrow canyons slice through masses of grayish white limestone rock, remnants of a huge inland sea that covered the region during the Cretaceous period 100 million years ago. Soils are shallow, rocky, and often interrupted by expanses of exposed bedrock. Low hills rise beyond the canyons, and elevation on the plateau varies from 290 meters at the confluence of the Devils River and the Rio Grande, to 400 meters along the canyon rim of the Pecos River. Although all rock art sites examined in this research are located north of the Rio Grande, the lower Pecos cultural area extends into Mexico (Turpin 1995), where the topography is somewhat different. Plains south of the Rio Grande are dissected by north-trending intermittent streams originating in the Serranias de los Burros, a mountain range

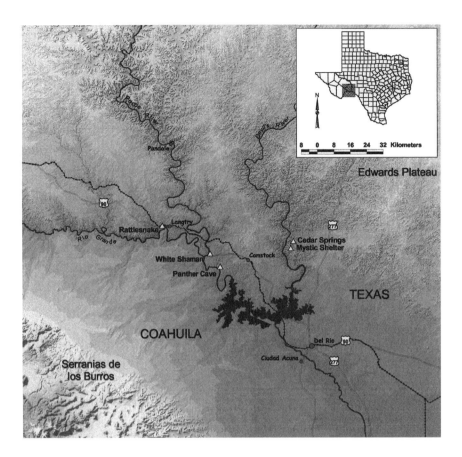

FIG. 2.1   The lower Pecos River region of southwest Texas and northern Mexico. Map by Michael Crow.

rising to almost 1,524 meters within 100 kilometers of the Rio Grande.

The region encompassing southwestern Texas and northeastern Mexico has a semiarid, subtropical climate with dry winters and hot summers (Golden, Gabriel, and Stevens 1982; Norwine 1995). It lies at the crossroads of two great climatic regimes of the continent— between the humid East and arid West, and between the seasonal midlatitude regimes to the north and winterless tropical climes to the south (Norwine 1995:140). Because of its position at a climatic crossroads, the lower Pecos experiences extreme annual variability in climate, characterized by frequent and unpredictable drought. In fact, it has more variability in rainfall than any other semiarid region in the world except northeastern Brazil (Norwine 1995:140). The immediate study area has an average annual rainfall of 44 centi-meters and averages three hundred frost-free days per year (Office of the State Climatologist 1987). Most precipitation occurs in two peaks, one in spring (April–May) and one in early fall (September–October). This bimodal rainfall pattern is distinct for the Chihuahuan Desert/Trans-Pecos region, which otherwise has a single summer monsoonal precipitation peak (Schmidt 1995).

Although the area has a desertlike appearance, the regional vegetation is actually characteristic of a savanna, defined as a tension zone between shrub or woodlands and grass-lands (Archer 1990; Archer et al. 1998). Climate changes or local land management practices may favor woodlands or grasslands. Grasslands were more widespread in the region before the extreme overgrazing of the late nineteenth century and the suppression of fire (Dering 1979). In his journal detailing the exploration of a new trade route between St. Louis, Missouri, and Chihuahua, Mexico, William Whiting noted the presence of grasslands that are no longer in existence today. As he approached the divide between the Devils and Pecos Rivers, Whiting (1938 [1849]:340) described the area as a succession of valleys and hills, "the valley covered with luxuriant crops of fine grass and the hills no longer obstructed by the limestone bluffs which hindered our march yesterday." Whiting is most likely speaking of the Blue Hills located just north of Comstock, Texas. Today the region is covered primarily by woody vegetation, and grasses are sparse.

The kinds of plants and animals present in the lower Pecos region are influenced by its position at the junction of the Tamaulipan, Balconian, and Chihuahuan Biotic Provinces (Blair 1950). To the east, vegetation is dominated by the mesquite–blackbrush acacia, shortgrass savanna that is typical of southern Texas (Blair 1950; Hatch, Gandhi, and Brown 1990). About twenty kilometers north of the Rio Grande, vegetation grades into the juniper-oak, shortgrass savannah associated with the Edwards Plateau (Amos and Gehlbach 1988; Hatch, Gandhi, and Brown 1990). To the west, vegetation rapidly becomes more xeric in character, dominated by the sotol-lechuguilla-creosote bush vegetation that is typical of the lower canyonlands of the Devils River, the Pecos River, and the Rio Grande. These latter taxa are commonly associated with the Chihuahuan Desert (D. Brown 1982).

Despite the fact that the region is technically a savanna, during the last hundred years woody plants have spread and now dominate the vegetation in most upland areas (fig. 2.2). These include mesquite (*Prosopis glandulosa*), several species of acacia (*Acacia* spp.), whitebrush (*Aloysia gratissima*), Texas persimmon (*Diospyros texana*), blue sage (*Salvia ballotiflora*), lotebush (*Ziziphus obtusifolia*), various buckthorns (*Condalia* spp.), and spiny hackberry (*Celtis pallida*). Creosote (*Larrea tridentata*) and ceniza (*Leucophyllum frutescens*) are prominent in many areas. Along the upper reaches of canyons, succulents and rosette-stemmed evergreens are also common, including prickly pear and tasajillo (*Opuntia* spp.), several yuccas

FIG. 2.2   View of the Rio Grande near Langtry, Texas. Photograph by J. Phil Dering.

(*Yucca* spp.), and lechuguilla *(Agave lechuguilla)*. Small trees are confined to narrow canyons or creek terraces. Littleleaf walnut *(Juglans micro-carpa),* several species of oak *(Quercus* spp.), Mexican ash *(Fraxinus greggi),* and Texas persimmon *(Diospyros texana)* are a few of the more prominent tree resources located in the canyons. Stands of huisache *(Acacia farnesiana)* and mesquite *(Prosopis glandulosa)* are located on terraces associated with San Pedro Creek.

The fauna of the region reflect a mix of animals from subtropical and temperate climes. Inventories associated with Amistad National Recreation Area have recorded sixty species of mammalian vertebrates, including ringtail cats, javelina, jackrabbits and cottontails, raccoons, whitetail deer, and porcupines (Ditton and Schmidly 1977). Mountain lion and black bear occasionally visit the region. A brief environmental study associated with the construction of Amistad Dam noted fifty-two species of amphibians and reptiles (Raun 1966); the region is frequented by snake collectors in search of such rare endemic species as the Trans-Pecos kingsnake. Vertebrate remains have been recovered from several archaeological sites in the region, providing an inventory of the kinds of animals that lived in the region over the past several thousand years. For example, at Hinds Cave, Lord (1984) identified sixty vertebrate taxa, including deer, pronghorn antelope (not seen in the area today), rabbits, birds, lizards, snakes, and fish. The faunal record from Hinds Cave indicates that from the Early Archaic through the Late Archaic (9000–1200 B.P.) species composition of vertebrate fauna did not change noticeably (Lord 1984). As Saunders (1986) noted, small game (mostly birds, rodents, snakes, and lizards), supplemented infrequently by deer, have always provided most of the meat for the region's aboriginal inhabitants.

Prehistoric Environment and Human Occupation

Archeologists and geologists have conducted several studies of the depositional history of river terraces and rockshelters or caves, assembling much information regarding past cultures and environments of the region. We know from twelve-thousand-year-old deposits at Bonfire Shelter (near Langtry) that an extinct species of bison roamed the region near the end of the relatively cool Pleistocene; shortly after that time bison disappeared. Supporting data indicate that the environmental history for the past ten thousand years is best described as having varied between "hot and dry" and "hotter and drier."

An unpredictable semiarid climate, shallow soils, and deep canyons with narrow terraces prone to catastrophic floods are conditions that limit the means by which indigenous people can live off the land. For this reason, people who lived in the lower Pecos were hunters of game, gatherers of wild plants, and fishers during the entire history of the region. Unlike areas to the south and west, areas that actually had less (but more predictable) rainfall, farming was seldom, if ever, practiced in the region. Groups who make a living by hunting, gathering, and fishing are usually described as hunters and gatherers, or foragers.

Foragers in arid lands usually live in small groups, travel long distances carrying few possessions, and change residence frequently. Therefore, the archaeological evidence left behind by foragers is relatively limited when compared to that of agricultural societies that live in villages or cities. The archaeological assemblages of the lower Pecos stand out as a major exception to this rule. Archaeological sites here are rather spectacular because so many are located in dry rockshelters or caves, which preserve otherwise perishable paintings, wooden implements, and plant fiber artifacts such as baskets and nets. In the lower Pecos

FIG. 2.3 Eagle Cave rockshelter located in Mile Canyon near Langtry, Texas. Photograph by J. Phil Dering.

there are more than two hundred rockshelter sites, most of which contain archaeological deposits; no other region in the Americas is known to contain so many well-preserved hunter-gatherer sites in such a small area (fig. 2.3). Other types of archaeological sites located beyond the canyons in open settings include burned rock middens, large accumulations of burned and fractured rock, where foods were cooked in earth ovens that used rocks as heating elements; quarry sites where stone for tools was collected; and campsites marked by small hearths or concentrations of chipped stone debris, the result of tool-making activities.

Archaeologists working with geologists and botanists have provided a history of environment and human occupation in the region. (See table 2.1 for a summary of cultural chronologies from the Lower Pecos.) Chronology of the lower Pecos region has received much attention—a result of excellent preservation, an influx of research funds associated with construction of Amistad Reservoir, and the presence of deeply stratified sites associ-ated with the Rio Grande and the Devils and Pecos Rivers. Turpin (1991) recorded 268 radiocarbon ages within or immediately adjacent to the lower Pecos River region on the U.S. side of the border. Only limited research has been conducted south of the Mexican border into the southern reaches of the lower Pecos cultural area.

PALEOINDIAN TO LATE PALEOINDIAN PERIOD (14,500–8500 B.P.)

Little is known about the region from the earliest part of this period, at the end of the Ice Age. At Cueva Quebrada (41VV162A) on the Pecos River, burned Pleistocene mammal bones with butchering marks were recovered in association with ten chipped stone flakes and a Clear Fork gouge, a stone tool probably used for woodworking. Charcoal from the same spatial context as the burned bone yielded dates ranging between 12,000 to 14,300 B.P. (Turpin 1991). Although Clear Fork gouges often occur in older deposits,

TABLE 2.1   Lower Pecos Regional Cultural Chronologies

YEARS B.P.	PERIOD	DIAGNOSTICS AND ROCK ART STYLES
500–present	Historic	Metal arrows; Historic style
1300–500	Late Prehistoric	Stemmed arrow points, ceramics
		Scallorn, Perdiz, Livermore, Toyah; Red Monochrome style
3000–1300	Late Archaic	Ensor, Frio; Red Linear style
		Marcos, Shumla
		Montell, Castroville, Marshall, Shumla; Pecos River style
6000–3000	Middle Archaic	Langtry, Val Verde, Arledge, Almagre; Pecos River style
		Pandale
8500–6000	Early Archaic	Baker, Bandy, Bell, Early Triangular: painted pebbles, clay figurines
		Angostura, Golondrina
9800–8500	Late Paleoindian	
11,000–9800	Paleoindian	Folsom, Plainview
		Clovis
14,500–11,900		None

the temporal connection between these early dates and the tools is at best tenuous, and confirmation of such an early occupation awaits better data.

The archeological record verifies human presence in the lower Pecos River region by 10,000 B.P. In a stratigraphic layer labeled Bone Bed 2 at Bonfire Shelter, extinct bison bones were recovered along with Folsom and Plainview dart points, which were made only during the Paleoindian period (Turpin 1991). This same deposit contained butchered remains of an estimated 120 to 200 *Bison antiquus,* a species of bison that has been extinct for thousands of years. These animals were stampeded over a cliff into the canyon below, and butchering marks are clearly visible on many of the bones. *Bison antiquus* bones were also recovered from the middle levels of Cueva Quebrada and the lowest level of Arenosa Shelter, both of which are roughly contemporaneous with Bone Bed 2.

Around nine thousand years ago, distinct changes in the lifeways of Paleoindian groups began to emerge. This change is well docu-

mented in the region's artifact assemblage. For example, dart point styles became more localized and diverse. Numerous Angostura and Golondrina points, typical of the Late Paleoindian period, have been recovered from the lower Pecos region, Rio Grande Plains, and the plains of northeastern Mexico (Epstein 1969; Hester 1995; Turpin 1995). Large animals of the Pleistocene became extinct, resulting in a Late Paleoindian subsistence economy that emphasized smaller game and more plant foods. This is best illustrated by analysis of a well-preserved hearth dating to 9000 B.P. in Baker Cave. The hearth contained sixteen plant taxa, eleven mammalian taxa, six fish, and eighteen reptiles (Hester 1983:140). The plant taxa included prickly pear, little walnut, sugar hackberry, mesquite, shin oak, and huajillo *(Acacia),* all of which are consistent with the semiarid savanna vegetation of modern-day conditions. Pollen studies from alluvial terraces of Arenosa Shelter, located on the Pecos River, have demonstrated that the environment was warming rapidly during this period. It is quite likely that the region was already experiencing modern climatic conditions about nine thousand years ago (Bryant and Holloway 1985).

EARLY ARCHAIC PERIOD (8500–6000 B.P.)

Although climate records are not very clear, it is apparent that the climate continued to dry out during this period (Bryant and Holloway 1985). The cultural record is vivid. The combination of a semiarid climate, deep canyons, and dry rockshelters in the lower Pecos River region has created near-perfect conditions for the best-preserved records of Archaic cultures in North America. Coiled and plaited basketry and various tool forms—including oval unifacial tools, manos, metates, and bedrock mortars—have been documented. Cordage made from lechuguilla and yucca was used in nets, snares, tools, and sandals. The technology of basketry and sandal manufacture was so similar to that documented at sites in northern Mexico that affiliation with groups to the south and west in Coahuila has been postulated (Andrews and Adovasio 1980; McGregor 1992).

During the Early Archaic, the foragers of the region often established residence in rockshelters. At Hinds Cave (41vv456) near the Pecos River, human activity areas within the shelter were well defined. Excavation of Hinds Cave revealed the presence of a latrine area; a floored area made of prickly pear pads; grass-lined pits; and oven areas surrounded by burned rock refuse (Lord 1984; Shafer and Bryant 1977).

Two types of portable art are known from the Early Archaic—painted pebbles (Parsons 1986) and clay figurines (Shafer 1975). Painted pebbles are thought to represent human figures, usually female. Clay figurines have exaggerated feminine attributes but are typically headless (Shafer 1975). Burial customs during the Early Archaic are poorly understood; however, a population of twenty-one indi-

viduals was recovered from Seminole Sink, a vertical-shaft cave associated with the Seminole Canyon drainage (Turpin 1988). All age groups and sexes were given the same type of burial, suggesting little social stratification.

Tools typical of the Early Archaic included Early Corner-Notched points such as Bell and Andice types, sequent flake unifaces, and Clear Fork gouges. These appear in deposits that date to the Late Paleoindian-Early Archaic periods and have been recovered from numerous sites, including Baker Cave (41vv216) in the lower Pecos River region (Turner and Hester 1999) and the Richard Beene (41bx831) site in south-central Texas (Thoms 1992).

MIDDLE ARCHAIC PERIOD (6000–3000 B.P.)

As population increased and the region became more arid, the people grew increasingly reliant on small animals and a greater variety of plant resources (Hester 1980). In the lower Pecos River region, the accepted diagnostic tool for the onset of the Middle Archaic is the Pandale dart point. Other stone tool markers of the period include Langtry and Val Verde points.

A definitive change in how people lived off the land is documented by the increased presence of earth ovens that used rocks as heating elements. By 6000 B.P. evidence from Hinds Cave demonstrates that earth ovens were used to cook lechuguilla *(Agave lechuguilla)* and sotol *(Dasylirion texanum)* (Dering 1999; Shafer and Bryant 1977). Similar ovens have been recorded from 5000 B.P. in Baker Cave by K. Brown (1991) who considered their presence to be an indication of a shift to less-desirable plant resources requiring more intensive labor input. Dering (1999) has argued that the spread of this labor-intensive technology is evidence that human populations in the region were having to work harder to extract enough food to survive in the region. Beginning in the Early Archaic and intensifying in the Middle Archaic, the population experienced at least seasonal, if not extended, periods of dietary stress or famine (Marks, Rose, and Buie 1988; Sobolik 1996).

By 4000 B.P. evidence of reduced mobility is suggested by increased diversity of lower Pecos artifact assemblages (Turpin 1995). Population densities increased as indicated by higher numbers of both "upland" and "lowland" sites in the lower Pecos River region (Marmaduke 1978). The apparent population increase was accompanied by the appearance of a complex, polychrome pictographic art form termed the Pecos River style. The walls of numerous rockshelters and cliff overhangs were used as canvases by lower Pecos artists during this period. These Pecos River–style murals are considered a hallmark of the Middle Archaic in the lower Pecos River region (Kirkland and Newcomb 1967).

LATE ARCHAIC PERIOD (3000–1300 B.P.)

At least two distinct subsistence and environmental shifts may have occurred during the nearly two-thousand-year span of the Late Archaic. The onset of the Late Archaic in the lower Pecos is marked by the return of bison to the region (Bement 1989; Turpin 1995). Bryant and Holloway (1985) documented a mesic interval marked by spikes in pine and grass pollen; this has been corroborated by pollen evidence recovered at the Diamond y Cienega in Pecos County (Hoyt 2000). This interval coincides with Bone Bed 3 at Bonfire Shelter, which contained the bones of more than eight hundred modern bison (*Bison bison*) dated to 2600 B.P. (Dibble and Lorrain 1968). Remains of bison have been recovered from similar (but poorly dated) contexts in Eagle

Cave, Arenosa Shelter, Castle Canyon, and Skyline Shelter (Turpin 1993). Environment of the period has been interpreted as cooler and wetter, promoting the expansion of grasslands that allowed bison to return to the region. Dibble and Lorrain (1968) and Turpin (1995) argued that people moved into the lower Pecos from the southern plains during this period, as suggested by a rise in the abundance of central Texas dart point styles (Montell, Ensor, Frio, Marshall, Castroville), the entry of a "fully developed" Red Linear rock art style, and a perceived shift from living in rockshelters to living in open site habitations.

During the final one thousand years of the Late Archaic, a steady increase in aridity is implied by a drop in percentages of grass and tree pollen and by bison disappearing from archeological deposits (Bryant and Holloway 1985; Turpin 1995). The time period is marked by the presence of the Shumla point type. Since the Shumla point has also been recovered from Cueva de la Zona in Mexico, it has been argued that people from the plains of Coahuila and surrounding mountains moved into the lower Pecos River region following the withdrawal of bison hunters (Turpin 1991, 1995).

Near the end of the Late Archaic, a change in burial practices occurred. This change is represented by a shift to bundle burials in dry rockshelters. A perceived shift to more intensive plant processing during the latter part of the Late Archaic is argued based on the presence of burned rock middens both inside and outside rockshelters (K. Brown 1991; Saunders 1986). Studies of desiccated human fecal remains, or coprolites, suggest that sotol and yucca became important dietary resources (Bryant 1974; Sobolik 1991). These plants provide a lower caloric yield than even *Agave lechuguilla* (Dering 1999).

LATE PREHISTORIC PERIOD (1300–500 B.P.)

The Late Prehistoric period is marked by the appearance of arrow points and presumably by use of the bow and arrow (Hester 1995; Turpin 1995). In the lower Pecos River region the earliest appearance of arrow points, the diagnostic artifact of the period, occurs around 1380 B.P. (Turpin 1991). To the south in Nuevo Leon, arrow points date to 1050 B.P. at La Calsada (Nance 1992) and to around 1200 B.P. at Cueva de la Zona. Many well-excavated sites do not contain Late Prehistoric deposits, due to changes in settlement patterns or to destruction of upper deposits by artifact hunters. Point types typical of the period in the lower Pecos include a variety of stemmed and unstemmed types, including Scallorn, Perdiz, Livermore, and Toyah.

Late Prehistoric burial customs included flexed interments, cremations, secondary disposal in vertical-shaft caves, and cairn burials. The Red Monochrome art style is linked to this time period (Turpin 1991). Bows and arrows are a pictographic element in the Red Monochrome pictographs, and the rock art style has been radiocarbon dated to approximately thirteen hundred years ago (Hyman and Rowe 1997; Ilger, Hyman, and Rowe 1994; Ilger et al. 1995).

A possible shift in subsistence is suggested by the documentation of tool kits associated with deer and particularly bison hunting (Black 1986: Johnson 1994). Perdiz arrow points and bone-tempered pottery, small end-scrapers, flake knives, beveled knives, perforators made of flakes, marine shell, and mussel shell typify assemblages from this horizon. The apparent emphasis on hunting exemplified by the tool kit suggests a reliance on more easily accessed food resources that do not require significant time or energy for processing. Therefore, it follows that these more accessible resources, most likely bison, may have returned to the region, thus bringing about this marked change in land use.

HISTORIC PERIOD (500 B.P.–PRESENT)

Cabeza de Vaca was the first European to enter the Rio Grande Plains and the coastal plain regions of Texas that are adjacent to the lower Pecos (Favata and Fernandez 1993). Castaño de Sosa's diary of 1590 provides us with the first European account of a traverse directly through the lower Pecos River region (Schroeder and Matson 1965). Spanish accounts often describe the lower Pecos region as sparsely inhabited; however, illegal slaving expeditions that preceded de Sosa's entry may have encouraged the Indians to avoid contact with Europeans.

Written records from the Protohistoric and early Historic periods (ca. A.D. 1500–1750) indicate that the region was populated by hunter-gatherer groups. No evidence of farming was noted by early observers. Cabeza de Vaca's observations emphasize heavy reliance on plant foods, especially roots (unidentified), prickly pear, and mesquite (Favata and Fernandez 1993). Farther west and south into Mexico, lechuguilla (mezcal) was an important staple. Reliance on mesquite, lechuguilla, grass seed, prickly pear tuna and nopales, and roots has been noted in historic records from northern Mexico, including Nuevo Leon and western Coahuila (Griffen 1969). In the early sixteenth century, when Cabeza de Vaca lived in the Rio Grande Plains and crossed southwestern North America, he seldom traveled a day without observing a settlement or other people, implying a fairly high population density (Favata and Fernandez 1993). This density was not observed by subsequent travelers, likely a result of depopulation due to the introduction of European diseases.

Cultural Ecology

Throughout prehistory, inhabitants of the lower Pecos lived in small groups often referred to as bands. Band size among foragers varies from single-family groups to as many as 150 to 200 people. The number of people constituting a band depends on several factors, such as the nature and quantity of available resources and the number of times a group changes residence. Analysis of archaeological sites suggests that band size among the lower Pecos hunters and gatherers was probably limited to about 25 to 30 individuals, with smaller family-sized bands of 10 to 15 individuals during the winter or lean seasons (Shafer 1988). Generally, band-organized societies are intensely egalitarian; all individuals of a particular age-sex category have equal access to prestige and resources. The concept of private property is typically alien to hunter-gatherers; sharing of virtually all resources is the rule.

Band mobility in the lower Pecos was determined by local resource availability, probably the availability of small and large game and to a lesser extent by plant resources (Dering 1999); residential camps were usually established around the most reliable water sources in the area (Shafer 1986, 1988). Although larger game animals, such as deer, provided a more substantial source of protein, they were not always available and were not a regular part of the diet. Coprolite and midden studies indicate that the people of the lower Pecos ate a wide variety of foods; no single resource occurred in sufficient abundance to be relied upon for a majority of the diet. Eating a wide variety of foods reduces the risk of starvation in an unpredictable environment (K. Brown 1991). Nonetheless, certain stable resources of the region made an important contribution to the diet and technology of the people. These resources included the xeric evergreen rosette plants—lechuguilla, sotol, beargrass, and several species of yucca—and various cacti, oaks, and grasses, as well as small game, such as fish, rabbits, and rodents. In addition to providing nutrients, agave, sotol, and yucca were used to make basketry, sandals, netting, and textiles, and for fuel, bedding, and floor covering. At least thirty-five wild plant foods and fifty to sixty types of small animals provided the caloric intake for the hunter-gatherers of the lower Pecos (Dering 1999:970; Lord 1984). This type of subsistence, practiced in marginal, high risk environments, is called a broad-spectrum economy.

In part because the lower Pecos foragers consumed a wide variety of plant foods and small game, and in part because the locally available resources were quickly exhausted, the people ranged widely across the landscape and changed residence often. Sobolik (1996) suggested a seasonal round that covers more than one hundred miles. Dering (1999) argued that the lower Pecos foragers moved frequently as they exhausted food and fuel resources in the narrow canyons. Although at this time no one can describe exactly how often the inhabitants moved or where their annual movements took them, clearly these people were quite mobile. They remained in one place long enough, however, to paint elaborate murals on the walls of canyons and rock-shelters. And they returned to these places repeatedly, to conduct rituals and to affirm other social contracts.

Rock Art of the Lower Pecos

During the Archaic period of the lower Pecos, walls of hundreds of rockshelters in the region were painted with an array of pictographic images. Although these rock paintings range in age from forty-two hundred years ago to the time of European contact, the vast majority of this art was produced during the middle to late Archaic period. Rock paintings within the

FIG. 2.4   Pecos River–style rock art, White Shaman (41VV124). Photograph by J. Phil Dering.

region have been categorized into four distinct and temporally successive styles—Pecos River, Red Linear, Red Monochrome, and Historic (Kirkland and Newcomb 1967).

The presence of an organic binder in the paints has allowed researchers to obtain radiocarbon ages through accelerator mass spectrometry (AMS). AMS dates for Pecos River–style art, the most ancient of the recognized styles, range from 4200 to 2950 B.P. (Chaffee, Hyman, and Rowe 1993, 1994; Hyman and Rowe 1997; Ilger et al. 1995; Russ et al. 1990); these dates place this rock art style within the latter part of the Middle Archaic, 4100 to 3200 B.P. My focus is almost exclusively on the Pecos River–style art, the most abundant and well-preserved art in the region (fig. 2.4).

FIG. 2.5   Red Linear–style rock art, Pressa Canyon (41VV201). Photograph by J. Phil Dering.

The Pecos River style consists of poly-chrome and monochrome anthropomorphic (humanlike) figures accompanied by an assortment of enigmatic designs. Anthropomorphs, ranging in height from approximately ten centimeters to eight meters, are variously depicted. For example, head and body shapes, ornamentation, size, and color vary between sites as well as within each rock art panel at a single location. Anthropomorph bodies are depicted facing forward with arms extending outward or with bodies in profile. Heads are either absent or depicted in a square, rectangle, oval, or other geometric form, or in a manner resembling a particular animal, such as a bird or feline. Frequently, anthropomorphs are depicted with head ornamentation, such as feathers or antlers, and with paraphernalia hanging from the arms or at the waist. Commonly found in association with these anthropomorphic figures are design elements such as atlatls (spear-throwers), spears and dart shafts, depictions of animals, serpentine lines, and geometric forms.

The two more-recent prehistoric rock art styles are dated on the basis of a single date for each: 1280 ± 150 B.P. for Red Linear and 1125 ± 85 B.P. for Red Monochrome (Ilger et al. 1995). The Red Linear style is characterized by small, red, stick figures of humans and animals engaging in group activities (fig. 2.5). Unlike the Pecos River style, Red Linear figures more closely resemble the human form. Individual sex can often be determined by the presence of either a phallus or a circle in the genital region. The Red Monochrome style consists primarily of frontally posed human figures associated with bows and arrows and realistically depicted animals in profile (fig. 2.6). Red Monochrome–style animals include turkeys, turtles, canines, felines, rabbits, fish, and deer. Red Monochrome panels are predominantly painted with pigments that produce red and orange hues. Although there is only one date available for this style, the presence of the bow and arrow in Red Monochrome rock art panels securely places it within the Late Prehistoric.

The Historic style has not been radiocarbon dated; but this style includes images

FIG. 2.6   Red Monochrome–style rock art, Painted Canyon (41vv78). Photograph by J. Phil Dering.

that reflect European contact (fig. 2.7). The Historic period in the lower Pecos began around 350 B.P. and extends to the present. Historic period rock art most commonly depicts missions, crosses, men on horseback, cattle, and robed figures.

LOWER PECOS
ROCK ART RESEARCH

In 1849 Captain S. G. French reported seeing Indian paintings near the mouth of the Pecos River. A few years later, a member of the Boundary Survey Commission also noted the paintings. Not until the 1930s, however, did serious efforts at recording and studying the art of the region begin. The most valuable early studies were conducted by Emma Gutzeit and Mary Virginia Carson for the Witte Memorial Museum, by Mr. and Mrs. Forrest Kirkland, and by A. T. Jackson (Turpin 1990).

In 1931 Gutzeit and Carson recorded 18 rock art sites, producing watercolor renderings of what they saw. A few years later, Forrest Kirkland, a commercial draftsman, and

his wife, Lula, began producing detailed watercolor renderings of all major sites in the region. The Kirklands' project was never completed due to Forrest's untimely death in 1942. Before he died, he managed to copy 91 pictograph and petroglyph sites across Texas, 43 of which are located in the lower Pecos River region. He was the first person to report stylistic and geographic variations in the art. Kirkland attributed this variability to different ethnic groups, naming them the Val Verde Dry Shelter and Val Verde Flooded Shelter cultures (Kirkland 1938). A. T. Jackson also began documenting rock art sites in Texas during the 1930s. In 1938 Jackson's photographs, sketches, and descriptions of 195 rock art sites, 35 of which are located in the lower Pecos, were published in *Picture-Writing of Texas Indians*. In his book, Jackson noted affinities between regions in Texas and the Plains, or the greater Southwest of the United States.

During the 1940s and early 1950s additional analyses and field studies were conducted by J. Charles Kelley and Herbert J. Taylor, Jr. Whereas Gutzeit and Carson

FIG. 2.7   Historic–style rock art, Vaquero Shelter (41vv77). Photograph by J. Phil Dering.

focused solely on recording the art through watercolor paintings and notes, Forrest Kirkland (1938), A. T. Jackson (1938), J. Charles Kelley (1950, 1971), and Herbert C. Taylor (1948, 1949a, 1949b) sought not only to record the art but also to suggest possible associations of the paintings with specific cultural groups who had inhabited the area in prehis-

toric times. Through the efforts of these individuals at least three styles were identified within the region: Pecos River style (labeled Val Verde Dry Shelter by Kirkland), Red Figure style (labeled Val Verde Flooded Shelter by Kirkland), and Historic style.

The planned impoundment of Amistad Reservoir in the 1960s generated a resurgence in rock art studies. During an extensive survey of the area, conducted by E. B. Jelks, J. A. Graham, and W. A. Davis, 200 archaeological sites were recorded on the Texas side of the Rio Grande, of which 49 were rock art panels. On the Mexican side of the Rio Grande, Rul and Taylor located 68 prehistoric sites, but only one of these sites contained rock art (Turpin 1990). Following the Amistad Reservoir survey, Terrence Grieder (1966) and David Gebhard (1965) photographed and artistically documented lower Pecos rock art sites, offering a relative sequence for pictographs in the major canyon systems of the area. Studying the wide variety of rock art within Seminole Canyon, Gebhard produced a detailed relative chronology. He defined six categories or types and four subphases, chronologically ordering the types based on stylistic criteria and superimposition.

A new version of rock art styles and chronologies was presented by W. W. Newcomb, Jr., in *The Rock Art of Texas Indians* (Kirkland and Newcomb 1967). Newcomb identified four rock art styles in the region; Pecos River, Red Linear, Red Monochrome, and Historic. Newcomb was the first to suggest that the polychrome and monochrome anthropomorphic figures, a dominant theme in the Pecos River style, were those of shamans. Using ethnographic analogy, Newcomb further developed an idea first presented by Campbell (1958) that attributed the Pecos River style to a shamanic religious system. J. Charles Kelley (1974) argued that the Pecos River style represents an artistic cult that developed in response to cultural emanations originating in Mesoamerica. Harry Shafer (1980) presented a compelling counter-argument. He suggested that "the similarities, if they do exist, between the lower Pecos shaman figures and iconographic motifs of Mesoamerica, may be merely the fortuitous result of different adaptive responses resulting

from a common desert culture base" (Shafer 1980:111).

Perhaps the most significant impetus for rock art research in the region was prompted by the Witte Museum of San Antonio in the early 1980s. The museum initiated an interdisciplinary effort to study and publicize prehistoric art of the lower Pecos region. Drawing on the skills of not only archaeologists but also paleobotanists, art historians, and social anthropologists, the Witte effort sought to interpret the material culture and investigate the lifestyle of the prehistoric hunter-gatherer inhabitants of the lower Pecos River region. Their endeavors resulted in the exhibit *Ancient Texans* at the Witte Museum and the publication of *Ancient Texans: Rock Art and Lifeways along the Lower Pecos* (Shafer 1986). It also led to a significant increase in public awareness of prehistoric art and a greater understanding of the hunting-gathering lifeways of the people who produced the art.

At about this same time, and with the advent of postprocessual archaeology, Solveig Turpin focused on the rock art of the lower Pecos region, authoring an extensive list of publications on the subject. Building on the works of Kirkland and Newcomb (1967) and Campbell (1958), Turpin identified additional elements associated with shamanic religious systems in the Pecos River–style art. Turpin also proposed a fifth, intrusive rock art style, Bold Line Geometric. She argued that Bold Line Geometric is "most clearly affiliated with the generic Desert Abstract styles of northern Mexico and the American Southwest" (Turpin 1995:551). Most recently, Turpin has recorded and documented Pecos River–style rock art sites in the Burro Mountains of Mexico, further extending the southern boundaries of the lower Pecos cultural area (1999). Her research represents a valuable contribution in lower Pecos archaeology.

Also in the 1980s Rice University initiated

the Pecos Project, an interdisciplinary project bringing together insights from anthropology, linguistics, psychology, and computer science in an effort to decode the lower Pecos symbolic system (Bass 1989). The Pecos Project was a computer-based venture aimed at identifying patterns in the rock art and decoding semantic meanings. Data generated during the project were subsequently interpreted by Patricia Bass, a member of the Pecos Project team, as evidence suggesting the possibility of male-associated and female-associated art (Bass 1989, 1994). Prior to Bass's research, interpretations of lower Pecos art tended to be rather androcentric; focusing on "man-the-hunter" or "man-the-shaman." Bass (1994:69) has argued for a "restructuring of the data to produce a de-gendered or more inclusive interpretation of this corpora of rock art."

A significant breakthrough in rock art research occurred in the late 1980s within the field of chemistry—the ability to radiocarbon date pictographs. Marvin Rowe and students working in his lab at Texas A&M University developed a method for obtaining AMS radiocarbon dates for rock art that required taking only a small sample of the paintings. Using this method, radiocarbon dates have been obtained for the Pecos River, Red Linear, and Red Monochrome rock art styles (Chaffee, Hyman, and Rowe 1993, 1994; Hyman and Rowe 1997; Ilger, Hyman, and Rowe 1994; Ilger et al. 1995; Russ et al. 1990). Before this breakthrough, rock art was largely disregarded by archaeologists because there was no sure way to place the art into a temporal context nor to assess its association with other material remains at an archaeological site. Marvin Rowe and his research team are now dating prehistoric art from around the world.

A few years later, DNA was extracted from the Pecos River–style rock art and subjected to polymerase chain reaction (PCR) and phylogenetic DNA analysis. Results of these analyses indicated that the organic binder in the paint was from a hoofed mammal, probably a deer or a bison (Reese et al. 1996). Mawk (1999) attempted to confirm the results of Reese et al. (1996) for the presence of artiodactyl DNA in Texas rock paintings but was unable to duplicate their findings. Although Mawk was unable to identify the presence of artiodactyl DNA in the rock paintings, experiments with paint-making using ingredients and natural resources available in the region during the Archaic period demonstrate that deer bone marrow would have made an effective binder. These replicative experiments revealed that mineral pigments and deer bone marrow, when combined with emulsifiers from yucca root and water, make an excellent paint (Boyd 1993).

The wealth of information afforded in the art of the lower Pecos region has only begun to be tapped. Until recently and in keeping with the Western attitude toward art as non-utilitarian, archaeologists with few exceptions have neglected art as a source of data about prehistoric cultures. Morphy (1989) argued that the analysis of prehistoric art has been held up for two main reasons:

- Prehistorians have not adequately integrated art with other archaeological data and have failed to subject it to analogous methods of analysis.

- They have neglected to recognize the complex ways in which art can be integrated within the social and cultural fabric of society.

The research design I have developed over the past decade is presented in the next chapter. I hope it will be useful to scholars and students alike as they seek to integrate prehistoric art with other archaeological data and use this important data resource in the reconstruction of lower Pecos prehistory.

Three

DRAWING FROM THE PAST: RECORDING AND DESCRIBING ROCK ART

One of the most troubling problems in archaeology is to determine about what or in what manner did prehistoric people think. A fundamental challenge is to develop the theory, methodology, and tools to understand human cognition.

C. RENFREW AND E. ZUBROW, *The Ancient Mind: Elements of Cognitive Archaeology*

Systematic scientific studies of rock art have, I believe, been seriously compromised by the prevailing Western viewpoint of art as non-utilitarian. Most North American archaeologists, influenced by this contemporary concept of art, have failed to integrate pictographs and petroglyphs with other archaeological data. Over the span of several years, I have developed, modified, and implemented a research design that integrates rock art with other archaeological data and subjects it to analogous methods of analysis. This method is specifically designed to describe, explain, and infer behavior from rock art as a feature in the archaeological record that should be studied within the context of an archaeological site. Although the techniques I have used to record rock art have been refined through the years, the research design used to formulate hypotheses and explain the rock art has not changed.

Research Design

Pictographic panels painted along rock shelter walls and cliff faces are nonportable artifacts or features. A feature, a concentration of functionally and temporally related artifacts, is considered to be the archaeological reflection of some activity or set of activities (Hester, Shafer, and Feder 1997:44). Based on this definition, rock art, which is clearly the reflection of past cultural activity, should be classed as an archaeological feature and subjected to analogous methods of analysis. As such, it should be studied in the context of an archaeological site. A site is "any discrete, bounded location where humans lived, worked, or carried out a task—and where evidence of their behavior can be recovered by the archaeologist" (Hester, Shafer, and Feder 1997:44).

FEATURE ANALYSIS

I address each rock art panel as a single unit or composition. This is accomplished by drawing a scale color rendering of each rock art panel. I then analyze the pictographs contained within each panel in an effort to identify patterns in the archaeological record.

Defining what constitutes a "rock art panel," like an archaeological "site," can be problematic. Identifying a rock art panel as a discrete, bounded location where imagery appears imposes a Western conception of the use of space on non-Western behavior. Areas within a rockshelter that are not painted may be just as much a part of the planned composition as those that are painted. Natural features in the rock surface, such as cracks and crevices, rock protrusions, and mineral stains, are frequently incorporated into the composition and should be considered part of the rock art panel. Although I recognize the difficulties associated with defining what constitutes a panel, the production of full-panel renderings requires that there be a beginning and an end. A rock art panel, therefore, is defined as the imagery contained within or immediately adjacent to a rock shelter; or contiguous imagery located along a cliff face with no more than four meters between painted surfaces.

In some areas of the world, rock art researchers are able to trace rock paintings and engravings. In the lower Pecos this method is not suitable because of the fragile condition of the paintings and their limestone canvases. Any contact with a painting can cause the delicate surface to splinter, or spall off. Therefore, scale renderings—rather than tracings—are made of entire rock art panels. As renderings, they are not exact duplicates of the panel but renditions produced through a series of steps involving sketching, photographing, and painting. Some rock art panels in the lower Pecos measure more than seven-by-seventy meters and contain hundreds of images. Although

scale renderings are very time consuming, the benefits of producing them are immeasurable. The researcher—no longer overwhelmed by the art, but familiar with it—becomes aware of each pictographic element and its spatial relationship to other elements in the panel. Subtleties that cannot be captured on film can be documented and included in the rendering. Photographic documentation tends to remove the researcher from the subject. No matter how much time I spend analyzing a photograph, if I do not sketch the art, I do not "know" the art. Elizabeth Wayland Barber eloquently expresses the benefits of this approach in her study of another aspect of material culture—textiles:

> I inspected photographs of the Venus Lespugue a dozen times, but it was not until I made my own tracing that I noticed the marks showing that the strings of her string skirt were fraying at the bottom, telling me that the sculptor knew of string made from twisted fiber twenty thousand years ago. The act of drawing forced me to pay minute attention to every tiny detail of the statuette for the first time. Similarly, it was not until I decided to color by hand my photocopies of all the known Mycenaean frescoes showing clothing that I began to appreciate how frequently a particular border pattern occurred. . . . Once we have located a good source of evidence, we need to sharpen our ability to make the most of what is there. The first step, in my experience, is to trick oneself into focusing on every part of the data. *Draw it, count it, map it, chart it,* and if necessary (or possible) *re-create it.* (Barber 1994:295)

Drawing and painting each pictographic element in the rock art panel not only increases awareness of imagery content but also helps identify variations and consistencies in artistic styles and recurring patterns in the art. For the purposes of this study, I define an "element" as a single pictographic component of a rock art panel, such as an anthropomorph, an animal, a spear-thrower, or a geometric form. Data collected on elements during production of the renderings are used to identify patterns or "motifs," which I define as recurring themes in the rock art that contain two or more pictographic elements. Subsequently, the distribution of pictographic elements and motifs across the landscape can be documented, noting their presence or absence within a canyon, between canyons, and among the major river systems in the region. The resulting distributional analysis of rock art is invaluable in identifying repeated associations of pictographic elements at various sites and in determining patterns of land use in the archaeological record.

FORMULATING AND TESTING
THE HYPOTHESES

Formulating a hypothesis to explain patterns identified during the feature analysis requires both formal knowledge and development of data correlates. This step begins with a careful and thorough study of ethnographic literature. First, I review the role of visual imagery, such as pictographs, sculptures, architecture, and so on, in indigenous societies around the world. Second, I conduct a more intensive review of ethnographic and ethnohistoric accounts of hunting-gathering societies located within arid environments similar to the area of the lower Pecos River region in Texas. Finally, the most thorough review of the ethnographic and ethnohistoric literature is focused on the regions of northern Mexico and the southwestern United States. This stage involves identifying and documenting patterns or motifs in the ethnographic literature. I define an ethnographic motif as a recurring theme in the ethnographic literature of two or more societies that contains similar components or ideas. Ethnographic data collected

during the review and patterns identified during the feature analysis of pictographs are used to formulate hypotheses regarding the meaning and function of the rock art.

The hypotheses are then assessed within the context of other aspects of regional material culture. Examining the art in conjunction with the artifacts recovered from the site itself aids in the explanation of both assemblages. Cable-like arguments are developed by intertwining distinct, separate strands of evidence. These separate strands of evidence come from areas such as the social and biophysical environment, animal behavior, and cognitive neuroscience. These strands can be either mutually reinforcing or mutually constraining. When each strand points to the same conclusion, they are mutually reinforcing; they are mutually constraining when certain strands result in the exclusion of a specific conclusion or whole classes of conclusions (Lewis-Williams 1995a).

Rock Art Recording and Data Collection

As a professional artist, I began recording rock art in the lower Pecos River region in the summer of 1989. At this early stage in my understanding of the art, my method consisted simply of sketching, photographing, and measuring isolated elements, and identifying motifs, operating under the assumption that each site contained a random assortment of rock art imagery. I soon recognized that the placement of imagery on the shelter walls was not random but patterned.

With this new insight, I realized the importance of studying the panels as compositions rather than focusing on isolated motifs. I began producing scale renderings of entire panels in the fall of 1991, using photographs and copies of watercolor paintings produced by Forrest Kirkland in the 1930s. After 1991 the renderings were produced using only photographs and sketches of the art. My goal in producing the renderings has not been to replicate the rock art in exacting detail, which would be time-consuming and cost prohibitive were it even possible. I produced the renderings to identify relationships of pictographic elements within a panel, to compare and contrast the pictographs at each site with others in the region, and to consider placement of the art across the landscape and within its archaeological context.

As my understanding of the pictographs increased, so did my questions. With this came more sophisticated methods for recording the rock art and collecting data from each of the archaeological sites. In 1997 I developed eight recording forms to be used in the field for documentation and analysis (see appendix). The recording methods and forms proved to be beneficial in addressing some of these new questions. As with any scientific endeavor, they are likely to undergo further refinement as new questions emerge.

FIELD PROCEDURES

Recording rock art at an archaeological site, in addition to other relevant data pertaining to the site itself, requires careful and extensive documentation. It also requires spending a few days to several weeks at each site. The field protocol and forms I developed for the project are discussed below. Examples of reporting forms are provided in the appendix.

STEP 1: SITE FORM. The site form, containing general site information, is completed immediately after reaching the site. This form is basically a modified version of the State of Texas Archeological Site Form and the Texas Parks and Wildlife Department's form used to record information about rock art sites.

STEP 2: PHOTO REFERENCE FORM. This form, adapted from the Rock Art Photo Reference Form developed by the Texas Parks and Wildlife Department, is used to keep an accurate record of all photographs. A photo reference numbering system is developed and maintained throughout the recording session.

STEP 3: ROCK ART RECORDING FORMS. Six forms are used to document specific pictographic elements at each rock art site. Each element is counted, and examples of each are documented on the recording forms. Pictographic elements are drawn and measurements are noted next to the drawing. A Munsell Color Guide is used to determine the appropriate color code for each figure; the code is then recorded with the corresponding drawing. Detailed written descriptions of the pictographs and all related pictographic elements are also recorded. The six rock art recording forms are

1. *Zoomorphs.* This form is divided into sections for different types of animals commonly represented in rock art—deer, canines, felines, birds, and reptiles. If other zoomorphs are identified, they are documented on a separate page and attached to this form.

2. *Centrastyled Anthropomorphs.* Anthropomorphic figures that are often polychromatic and that have some form of design along the central area of the body or decoration along the exterior lines of the body are considered centrastyled, or skeletonized, anthropomorphs (fig. 3.1). I use the terms centrastyled and skeletonized interchangeably. The term "skeletonized" typically is used to refer to images depicted in X-ray fashion, revealing the inner, skeletal image of the figure being illustrated. I use the term to include not only the physical but also the spiritual manifestation of

FIG. 3.1 Panther Cave (41vv83). Centrastyled (skeletonized) anthropomorphic figure. Scale 1cm ≈ 30cm.

the subject. The spiritual essence of the subject is illustrated in indigenous art by decorating the central portion of the body with lines or bands. These designs are not meant to resemble the human skeleton—the physical aspect—but to represent the inner, spiritual aspect of the subject. Skeletonization is discussed in greater detail in chapter 4.

3. *Noncentrastyled Anthropomorphs.* All anthropomorphic figures that lack decoration down the central section of the body or designs along the exterior lines of the figure are considered noncentrastyled. In the lower Pecos, these are typically monochromatic and smaller in size than centrastyled anthropomorphs.

4. *Therianthropes.* Therianthropes are anthropomorphs with animal characteristics, such as antlers, wings, furlike fringe, and so on. They are typically skeletonized and are frequently elaborate polychromatic figures.

5. *Handprints and Geometrics.* Positive and negative handprints, although not a common element in lower Pecos rock art, are present in some of the rock art panels. Geometrics are a fairly common pictographic element.

6. *Subject.* This form is used as an addendum to the other forms when more space is needed.

STEP 4: FIELD SKETCHES. Sketches are made of complex areas and faint images within the panel that may not be clearly depicted in photographs. These sketches, along with site photographs (step 5), are used to develop full-panel renderings. Sketches are produced on acid-free paper and include measurements, Munsell color codes, and a detailed written description. Each subject of a field sketch is also photographed.

STEP 5: PHOTOGRAPHY. Site photographs include individual pictographic elements and motifs; meter-by-meter units of the entire panel; general site overviews; and local vegetation and landscape. All photographs are recorded on a reference form. When a rock art panel is photographed, the archaeological site number, panel unit number, and scale are indicated on a menu board that is included in each photograph.

LABORATORY PROCEDURES

One problem that plagues archaeologists is that rock art cannot be excavated, labeled, bagged, and transported to the lab for analysis. With proper field methods, however, the rock art can be taken back to the lab for analysis in the form of sketches, photographs, extensive notes, and measurements. The rock art panel can be reconstructed in the lab from data collected in the field.

STEP 1: ORGANIZING SLIDES. Site number, photo reference number, and unit number (when applicable) are noted on all slides. Slides are then placed in archival-quality plastic slide sleeves.

STEP 2: PRODUCING THE RENDERING. Pastels and Prismacolor professional-quality soft colored pencils are used to re-create the full-panel renderings on 100 percent rag vellum or acid-free paper. Panel unit slides are projected onto the paper and lightly copied using a soft pencil. The surface of the paper is toned with pastels to resemble the color of the shelter wall. This involves grinding pastel pigments to a fine powder, then lightly rubbing the powder into the surface of the paper using a soft cloth, tissue, or cotton ball. Detailed images are then added using the colored pencils, with color selection determined by the Munsell color codes recorded in the field. Sketches and photographs of individual elements are used to add further detail from complex or faint areas of the panel. Since pastels and colored pencils are easily erased, adjustments and corrections can be made to the rendering with relative ease.

Producing a rendering is an ongoing, long-term process. Subsequent trips to a site inevitably reveal new data or necessary adjustments to existing images. Different lighting conditions, better weather conditions, more time spent at a site, improved photographic images, and even fewer annoying gnats can result in discoveries of previously unseen subtleties in the rock art. In sum, no rendering can ever be considered totally complete.

STEP 3: DATA ANALYSIS. Once the majority of the images have been rendered and the rendering itself has been refined, pictographic elements are counted and verified against counts recorded on rock art recording forms, with corrections made as needed. Data collected from all the sites in the study are then compared. Because rock art panels are not equal in size or complexity, a simple numeric comparison of sites cannot accurately reflect the density of pictographic elements within each panel. Determining precise counts of pictographic elements is also extremely difficult. Many of the images are faint, damaged, completely destroyed, or lost under other imagery. Although every effort is made to treat the data as accurately as possible, complete reconstruction of the imagery contained in the panel is simply not possible.

Analysis of Five Lower Pecos Rock Art Panels

The research design and recording techniques discussed above were used in documenting and analyzing five Pecos River–style rock art panels—Rattlesnake Canyon (41vv180), White Shaman (41vv124), Panther Cave (41vv83), Mystic Shelter (41vv612), and Cedar Springs (41vv696). These rock art panels were selected based on geographic location and their relatively high degree of preservation. They are located within rockshelters found along four major drainage systems that feed into the Rio Grande: Rattlesnake Canyon, Pecos River, Seminole Canyon, and Devils River (see fig. 2.1). The counts given for each element are approximations; an exact count is impossible due to damaged panels, overpainting, weathering, and observation conditions. Improved photographic image-enhancement technology is certain to result in slightly different counts than what I present here; however, it is unlikely that any technology will be able to capture all the original imagery painted on shelter walls.

The referents I have adopted for pictographic elements—such as "feather headdress," "stafflike object," and so on—are not intended to be functional explanations or interpretations of the rock art; they are used only as descriptors. Too often, terminology associated with pictographic elements becomes accepted as an interpretation of the art, when in fact its original significance may have been quite different from the referent being used. To avoid confusion, I do not use the term "therianthrope" when referring to anthropomorphs with animal attributes. Instead, I discuss these within the context of other anthropomorphic figures and refer to them as "winged anthropomorphs," "rabbit-eared anthropomorphs," "antlered anthropomorphs," and the like.

Placement of pictographs in rock art panels is described from the viewer's perspective—that is, facing the panel. Reference to the right- or left-hand side of anthropomorphic figures, however, is from the perspective of the painted figure.

RATTLESNAKE CANYON (41VV180)

This site is located in a deeply incised canyon near the town of Langtry, Texas, about 275 meters from the Rio Grande. The entire wall of this small, southwest-facing shelter is covered with pictographs, and the bulk of the paintings are Pecos River style. Dimensions of the painted surface are approximately 3 by 24 meters (height by length). As with many lower Pecos rock art panels, Rattlesnake Canyon is a complex composition containing hundreds of pictographic elements (plate 1). The pictographs are in fair condition; shelter flooding has damaged the lower section of the panel and spalling has caused serious damage to its far right side. Flooding also removed the majority of shelter archaeological deposits, with the exception of remnant burned rock scatters. Primary pictographic elements identified at Rattlesnake Canyon are discussed below.

ANTHROPOMORPHS. One of the most striking aspects of this panel is the number of dichromatic and polychromatic centrastyled anthropomorphic figures. At least fifty-eight of the sixty-three anthropomorphs identified in this panel are skeletonized. Predominant colors are red and black, but various shades of yellow and orange are also present. Four distinctive characteristics are associated with these figures. First, approximately seventeen

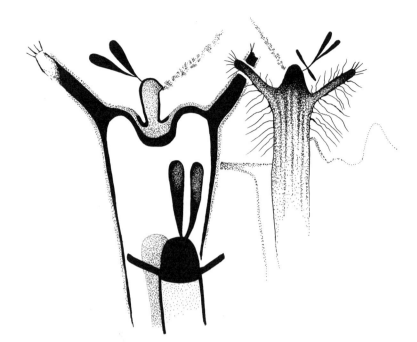

FIG. 3.2 Rattlesnake Canyon (41VV180). Rabbit-eared anthropomorphs. Scale 1cm ≈ 15cm.

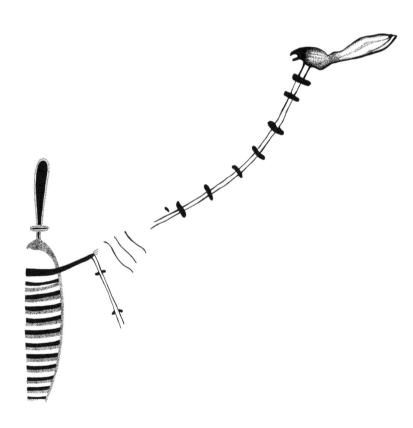

FIG. 3.3 Jackrabbit Shelter (41VV576). Rabbit-eared element identified in Painted Canyon west of the Pecos River. Scale 1cm ≈ 20cm.

of the anthropomorphs have either a single or dual feather headdress or rabbit ears (fig. 3.2). Because this same pictographic element is associated with a rabbit's head in another rock art panel in the area (fig. 3.3), I refer to these as rabbit ears throughout the book. The rabbit ears appear on figures found within all areas of the panel and at all levels of superimpositioning (that is, figures with rabbit ears are superimposed over other figures with the same design).

Wings are the second characteristic of the

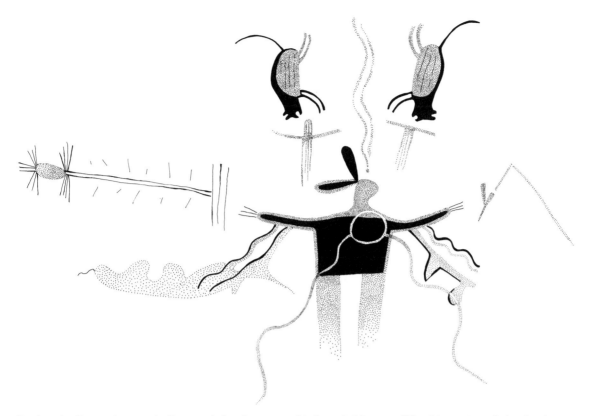

FIG. 3.4 Rattlesnake Canyon (41VV180). Centrastyled anthropomorphic figure holding a stafflike object in its right hand and an atlatl in its left hand. The anthropomorph is passing through an opening in a crenelated arch. Scale 1cm ≈ 14cm.

anthropomorphs; at least twenty-one of the figures are winged. Nine of the winged figures do not have legs, and all the winged anthropomorphs are painted either horizontally or at an angle on the wall. None of the winged figures are depicted with rabbit ears. The third characteristic of the Rattlesnake Canyon anthropomorphs is their association with a stafflike object bearing an enlarged distal end (fig. 3.4). The anthropomorphs are "holding" this object in either their right or left hand. Although I describe these and other objects as being "held" by the anthropomorphs, they are actually only located near the right or left hand. The enlarged distal end is depicted in a variety of ways and is stylistically comparable to the anthropomorph with which it is associated. The fourth characteristic is the association of anthropomorphs with atlatls (fig. 3.4). At least fifteen of the anthropomorphs are holding atlatls in either their right or left hand; none

of the winged anthropomorphs are associated with this pictographic element. At least four skeletonized anthropomorphs have been impaled by a spear. These figures are winged and are depicted horizontally on the right end of the panel, as opposed to the vertical position of the nonimpaled anthropomorphs located throughout the panel.

ZOOMORPHS. The number of animal figures depicted in the panel is low compared to the number of anthropomorphs. There are approximately four felines and three birds. The birds are located near the center of the panel, whereas the felines are located on the left side of the panel. Although numerous serpentine or crenelated lines appear throughout the paintings, there are no distinguishing attributes that can be used to positively identify them as snakes.

GEOMETRICS AND OTHER ENIGMATIC FIGURES. Crenelated or serpentine lines are depicted using a single color or with several colors. At least three of the more complex images consist of crenelated lines that form an arch. At the top of the arch is a circle or a break in the lines. Each of these crenelated arches is associated with one of the skeletonized anthropomorphs, which are painted either above, below, or behind the crenelation (fig. 3.4). These figures are located within the left section of the panel.

More than one hundred straight lines resembling spears or feathered darts are clustered around the bodies of various anthropomorphs and amoeba-like figures. There is also a cigar-shaped figure approximately two and a half meters long in the central section of the panel. At the far right end of the panel, a large cluster of concentric circles is painted in black and red. The circle is impaled by a spear or dart and is surrounded by the impaled, winged figures.

WHITE SHAMAN (41VV124)

The White Shaman site is located in a small, southwest-facing shelter high on a bluff overlooking the Pecos River near its confluence with the Rio Grande. Dimensions of the pictographic panel within the shelter are four by eight meters (plate 2). The paintings, predominantly Pecos River style, are in fairly good condition, except for the lower portion of the panel, which has been damaged by sheep and goats rubbing against the paintings. The damaged section of the panel contains small linear images that are not discussed because they are very difficult to see. The majority of the paintings are in good condition and are included in the rendering. Although there are no sedimentary deposits in the shelter, some burned rock and midden debris are found in the talus slope below the shelter.

ANTHROPOMORPHS. Although small in comparison to other sites in the study, this panel contains more than thirty anthropomorphic figures, both centrastyled and non-centrastyled. Five black, noncentrastyled anthropomorphic figures with red heads extend the length of the panel. The figures are approximately the same size and are spaced fairly evenly apart. Associated with each of these anthropomorphs are long, slender, black objects with red tips. These objects are associated with the right and left hand of each anthropomorph (fig. 3.5).

At least ten anthropomorphs are impaled; seven of them are also skeletonized. Six of these impaled, centrastyled anthropomorphs are depicted upside down with "hair" falling downward. These figures have spears or feathered darts in each hand, but none of them are holding atlatls. Their bodies are frequently decorated with black dots.

Two headless, white, centrastyled anthropomorphs are located near the center of the panel; each has a black band running down the center of its body. One is outlined in red and has red lines decorating the body. The other is faded and less elaborately painted. At the left end of the panel are two antlered, centrastyled anthropomorphs. One of these figures is impaled and has two sets of antler racks on its head. The other antlered figure is painted in red and black; its antler tines are tipped with black dots. This figure is holding an atlatl in its right hand and a stafflike object with an enlarged, spinescent distal end in the left hand. It is the only figure identified at the site that has eyes. Eyes and other facial features are very rarely depicted in Pecos River–style rock art.

ZOOMORPHS. I have identified three impaled deer in the panel. One is located at the right end of the panel; another very small one is located near the center; the third is at the left end. All three are painted in red. The one to

FIG. 3.5 White Shaman (41vv124). Centrastyled, white anthropomorph associated with a black, noncentrastyled figure holding a torchlike object in each hand. Upside-down impaled anthropomorphs are located beneath the white figure.
Scale 1cm ≈ 12cm.

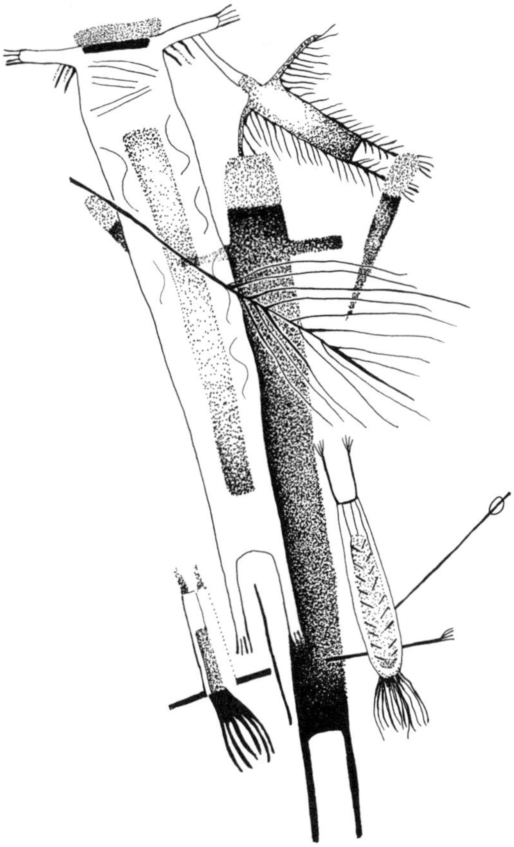

the left, which is covered in large black dots, is located just above the two antlered anthropomorphs.

GEOMETRICS AND OTHER ENIGMATIC FIGURES. There are well over one hundred dots in this panel. Although many of the dots are free-floating, just as many decorate figures in the panel. At least six red dots have been impaled with feathered darts or spears. Three of these are located at the far left end of the panel near the antlered figures. The other impaled dots are seen in the underbelly region of a large and enigmatic serpentlike figure located in the center of the panel. Two other enigmatic polychrome figures—not human, not animal—are also decorated with dots.

Crenelated lines are present, including a crenelated arch with an opening that extends down the center of the arch. The skeleton-

ized, antlered anthropomorph with dots on its tines is located in the central section of the arch. A white crenelated line runs the entire length of the panel and crosses over the top of the five black anthropomorphs discussed above. As best as can be determined, no pictographic elements superimpose this line. At the far left end of the panel, the white line changes to black.

PANTHER CAVE (41VV83)

Panther Cave is a large, west-facing rock-shelter located near the mouth of Seminole Canyon and within Seminole Canyon State Park. Pecos River–style paintings extend approximately six by forty meters along the back wall of the shelter (plate 3). Archaeological deposits exceeding two meters in depth have been severely impacted by recent activity. The once-extensive talus slope associated with the shelter was inundated following construction of amistad reservoir. Paintings on the exterior walls of the shelter are barely visible due to weathering. The paintings inside the shelter are in fair condition; however, serious damage has been caused by water seepage, mineral stains, insect burrowing, and spalling. The condition of the paintings and the extensive amount of superimpositioning made counting pictographic elements in this panel quite difficult.

ANTHROPOMORPHS. More than forty anthropomorphs are included in the Panther Cave panel, at least thirty of which are centrastyled. Depiction of anthropomorphs is quite diverse. Some are elaborately painted with two or more colors; others are less ornate. One notable attribute of the Panther Cave anthropomorphs is feather hipclusters. At least seven of the larger anthropomorphs located toward the right end of the panel have a cluster of what looks like feathers at the hip. Also depicted are one winged anthropomorph and one anthropomorph wearing a feather headdress. In contrast to Rattlesnake Canyon, no rabbit-eared anthropomorphs have been identified at Panther Cave.

ZOOMORPHS. At least seventeen impaled deer and eight felines have been identified in the Panther Cave panel. The felines, which are often quite large, are located throughout the panel and extend as much as three and a half meters in length. The deer are small, measuring approximately thirty centimeters in length, and are located near the right and left ends of the panel.

GEOMETRICS AND OTHER ENIGMATIC FIGURES. There are more than one hundred lines resembling feathered darts, most of which are located at the far right end of the panel surrounding an anthropomorph and a rounded, enigmatic, black and red figure. Just below the rounded figure are red and yellow

impaled dots and numerous impaled deer. Several impaled geometric forms that resemble a single-pole ladder are also located in this section of the panel.

Crenelated lines are located throughout the panel. In at least two instances, these lines form an arch. An opening or break in the crenelation is located in the center of the arch (fig. 3.6). At the far right end of the panel just beneath a very large feline is a third crenelated line that connects to a circle. There may be a mirror image of the crenelated line connecting to the other side of the circle, but this is yet to be determined. Numerous lines radiate upward from the circle. Located between the circle and the feline is a centrastyled anthropomorph.

MYSTIC SHELTER (41VV612)

Mystic Shelter is located in a small arroyo that feeds into the Devils River just south of Cedar Springs Canyon. The southeast-facing shelter consists of three levels, or tiers. The lowest level contains very little art—perhaps due to flooding—and the upper level contains no art. The majority of the rock art is contained within the second tier, which is high enough to be protected from flood waters. Measuring approximately five by twenty meters, the pictographic panel located within this section of the shelter contains predominantly Pecos River–style rock art; however, there are also numerous paintings identified as Red Linear style (plate 4). Because of water seepage, entire sections of the panel have been destroyed. Those sections not damaged by seepage are in excellent condition, but the likelihood of damage from further water seepage appears imminent. There are no sedimentary deposits at this site and no talus.

ANTHROPOMORPHS. More than forty anthropomorphs are in this panel. Extensive damage to the paintings suggests that numer-

Color Plates

PLATE 1   Rendering of Rattlesnake Canyon (41VV180).
Scale 1cm ≈ 80cm.

PLATE 2   Rendering of White Shaman (41VV124).
Scale 1cm ≈ 30cm.

PLATE 3   Rendering of Panther Cave (41vv83).
Scale 1cm ≈ 1.5m.

PLATE 4   Rendering of Mystic Shelter (41vv612).
Scale 1cm ≈ 50cm.

PLATE 5   Rendering of Cedar Springs (41vv696).
          Scale 1cm ≈ 1m.

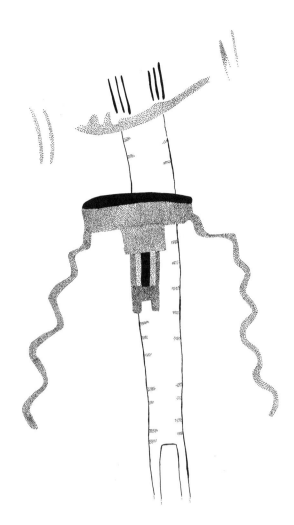

FIG. 3.6   Panther Cave (41vv83). Anthropomorph passing
through an opening in a crenelated arch.
Scale 1cm ≈ 14cm.

ous anthropomorphs may have been destroyed. At least three anthropomorphs are
holding a stafflike object with an enlarged,
spinescent distal end. Two antlered anthropomorphs are depicted at this site. One is polychrome—yellow, red, and black—with black
dots decorating its body. The tines of its red
antler rack are tipped in black. The other
antlered anthropomorph is dichromatic,
painted in yellow and red, and is located at the
far right end of the panel.

No fewer than fourteen anthropomorphs at
Mystic Shelter are impaled. At least four are
nonskeletonized and are depicted vertically on
the panel. The other ten impaled skeletonized
figures are depicted either upside down, horizontally, or at an angle.

ZOOMORPHS. Felines and deer are present
in the Mystic Shelter paintings. Four felines,
all depicted in a different fashion, are located
toward the right end of the panel. The largest
feline is approximately 3 meters long, with
red lines emanating from the nose and mouth.
Just beneath the large feline are two smaller
felines, approximately half the size of the one
above. The legs, tail, and claws of one of these
felines are detached from its body; the front
portion has been destroyed by water seepage,
so it is impossible to determine how the head
of the figure was originally illustrated. The
other feline is headless, but its appendages
are attached. The fourth feline is located at
the far right end of the panel near an antlered
anthropomorph; this feline's head is contorted
backward.

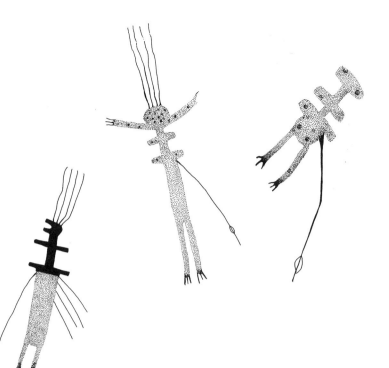

FIG. 3.7   Mystic Shelter (41vv612).
Impaled single-pole-ladder
anthropomorphs.
Scale 1cm ≈ 10cm.

The Mystic Shelter paintings also include five deer and a large horned serpent approximately 5.6 meters in length. The deer, all of which appear to be impaled, are located at the far left end of the panel. The horned serpent is painted red with a black line running down the top of its body. Alternating red and black dots decorate its underside. The right end of the serpent has been destroyed by water seepage.

GEOMETRICS AND OTHER ENIGMATIC FIGURES. Squares are located just above three anthropomorphic figures. Two of these squares have lines extending outward from the lower two corners. These squares are painted red, yellow, and orange.

A pictographic element resembling a single-pole ladder appears frequently throughout the panel; some are impaled and others are not. The single-pole ladders are located just to the right of the deer. These geometrics are associated with impaled skeletonized anthropomorphs. The impaled anthropomorphs

have bodies resembling the single-pole ladder (fig. 3.7).

Crenelated lines are present in all areas of the panel. Two crenelated arches with openings in the center are associated with anthropomorphs. Only one of the anthropomorphs is skeletonized.

CEDAR SPRINGS (41VV696)

This site is located within Cedar Springs Canyon approximately 900 meters above the Devils River. It is a large, southeast-facing shelter located just above the canyon floor. The back wall of the shelter is covered with Pecos River–style pictographs in fair condition. The painted surface is approximately 7 by 31 meters (plate 5). There are no cultural deposits in this shelter. Due to the shelter's low elevation, flooding has likely removed any accumulated deposits. Adjacent to the main Cedar Springs shelter is the Cedar Springs annex. Paintings in the annex are approximately 34.5 meters long and appear originally to have been joined with the paintings in the main shelter. With the exception of a few pictographs protected by a slight rock overhang, the majority of the paintings in the annex have been damaged or completely destroyed by exposure to the elements, mineral deposits, and spalling. Because the paintings in the main shelter and the annex appear to have been contiguous, they are discussed together.

The Cedar Springs rendering was the last one to be produced during this study, and the annex has not yet been rendered as a complete unit. Due to the poor condition of the pictographs, it has only been possible to sketch isolated sections of the annex paintings.

ANTHROPOMORPHS. One hundred and thirty-seven anthropomorphs have been identified in the paintings at Cedar Springs—85 in the main shelter and 52 in the annex. Of the 137 anthropomorphs, 88 are non-centrastyled and are less than 50 centimeters in height. The remaining anthropomorphs, which are skeletonized, range from approximately 30 centimeters to 5 meters in height. At least 20 skeletonized anthropomorphs are elaborately painted and adorned with animal attributes, such as antlers, bird heads, or fur. Twenty-nine of the anthropomorphs are centrastyled, but do not appear to have any animal attributes.

At least 4 of the anthropomorphs are antlered. Antler tines on 2 of the anthropomorphs are tipped in black; the third antlered figure has only the main beam tines tipped in black. The fourth antlered anthropomorph, located in the annex, does not appear to have any decorated tines. About 20 of the anthropomorphs are holding a stafflike object with an enlarged distal end in the left hand and an atlatl in the right hand. One anthropomorph is holding the stafflike object in its right hand rather than its left. Five occurrences of the stafflike object are not associated with anthropomorphs. One anthropomorph has large wings and a bird head. One or two have a feathered headdress. No impaled anthropomorphs have been identified at this site.

ZOOMORPHS. Deer, felines, and possibly 2 birds are present in the Cedar Springs paintings. There are at least 31 deer in the paintings at Cedar Springs, most of which are impaled. Ten deer have been identified in the main shelter, 9 of which are similarly depicted and located in the central section of the panel. These 9 deer are associated with an antlered anthropomorph. The tenth deer, which is very faded, is located in the left-hand section of the panel and is not depicted in the same manner as the other 9. Twenty deer, stylistically different from those in the main shelter, have been identified in Cedar Springs annex. For the most part, their bodies are short and fat; a few are more elongated.

At least 16 felines have been identified in the Cedar Springs paintings. Eleven are depicted with their heads contorted backward, mouths open, and impaled with a spear or feathered dart (fig. 3.8). These felines, located in the central section of the panel, are surrounded by the impaled deer. Also located in this section is a negative-painted feline with red lines emanating from its mouth and nose area. This feline is superimposed over the top of an antlered anthropomorph. Above the impaled deer and the felines is what appears to be an antlered feline; it is impaled and has its head contorted backward (fig. 3.9).

GEOMETRICS AND OTHER ENIGMATIC FIGURES. The paintings at Cedar Springs contain a plethora of geometric forms and enigmatic figures: Y-shapes, T-shapes, comb-shapes, U-shapes, amoeba shapes, and single-pole ladders. Each of these geometrics is associated with a specific anthropomorph. The

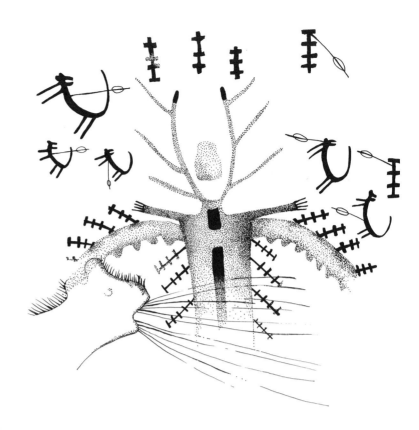

FIG. 3.8 Cedar Springs (41vv696).
Antlered anthropomorph with
main beam tines tipped in black
and surrounded by impaled
felines. Superimposed over the
antlered figure is a large feline.
Scale 1cm ≈ 13cm.

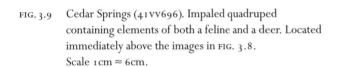

FIG. 3.9 Cedar Springs (41vv696). Impaled quadruped
containing elements of both a feline and a deer. Located
immediately above the images in FIG. 3.8.
Scale 1cm ≈ 6cm.

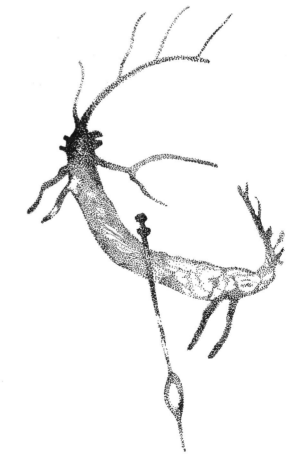

single-pole ladder forms are frequently impaled and located in the area of the impaled deer, impaled felines, and antlered anthropomorph (see fig. 3.8). There are also anthropomorphs with single-pole ladder bodies similar to those at Mystic Shelter.

More than one hundred lines resemble spears or feathered darts; most of these surround the body of an anthropomorphic figure. Crenelated lines—some monochrome and simple, others ornate and polychrome—are a frequently occurring pictographic element. There are two very elaborate crenelated arches with openings in the center. Beneath one of the arches is a skeletonized antlered anthropomorph; the other arch, which is inverted, is not associated with an anthropomorph. Other crenelated arches in the panel do not have openings in the center.

Large U-shaped elements, as well as crenelated figures resembling the letter W, are located in the annex. Other geometrics include grid patterns, dots, concentric circles, circles linked with lines, and nested curves. At least eight impaled black dots, four of which are very distinct, are located in the annex (fig. 3.10). The Cedar Springs paintings contain a wide variety of amoeba-like figures. One of these with animal characteristics is associated with at least three of the stafflike objects described above.

A Patterned Past: Distribution of Rock Art Elements

Primary pictographic element counts from each site were compared in order to identify patterns in the rock art (table 3.1). Analysis of these data revealed patterns in the distribution of specific pictographic elements. It also revealed "motifs," repeated themes or dominant features in the rock art that are composed of two or more pictographic elements.

PECOS RIVER–STYLE MOTIFS

Three of the primary or recurring motifs identified during this study are briefly described below. Motif A is discussed in chapter 4; Motifs B and C, in chapter 5.

MOTIF A. Elements of this motif include a crenelated arch with an opening in its center

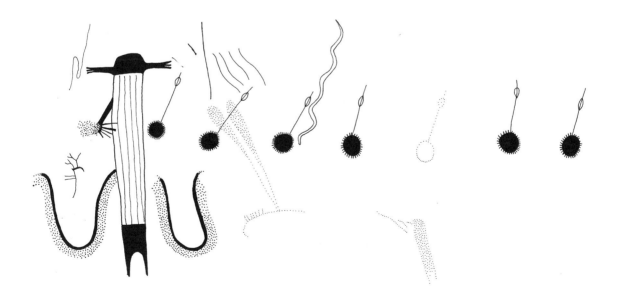

FIG. 3.10   Impaled black dots located in Cedar Springs annex (41VV696). Scale 1cm ≈ 14cm.

TABLE 3.1   Comparison of Pictographic Elements from Each Site

	RATTLESNAKE CANYON (41VV180)	WHITE SHAMAN (41VV124)	PANTHER CAVE (41VV83)	MYSTIC SHELTER (41VV612)	CEDAR SPRINGS (41VV6960)
ZOOMORPHS					
Felines	4	0	8	4	16
Deer	0	2	17	6	31
Birds	3	0	0	0	2
Horned serpents	0	0	0	1	0
ANTHROPOMORPHS					
Antlered	0	2	0	2	4
With rabbit ears	17	0	0	0	0
With feather headdress	1	0	1	0	2
Winged	21	0	1	0	1
With hipclusters	0	0	7	0	0
With stafflike object	8	1	12	3	20
Impaled	4	10	1	14	0
GEOMETRICS					
Impaled dots	0	6	15	0	8
Crenelated arch with opening	3	1	2	2	2

and a skeletonized anthropomorph located above, below, or behind the arch. The anthropomorph is either associated with a particular animal or its body has been adorned with animal attributes. This motif was identified at all five sites.

MOTIF B. Impaled deer, impaled dots, and antlered anthropomorphs with dots on the tips of their antler tines or decorating their bodies are elements of this motif. Although absent from Rattlesnake Canyon (41VV180), all three elements associated with Motif B were identified at Cedar Springs (41VV696) and White Shaman (41VV124). Two recurring elements of this motif were identified at Panther Cave (41VV83) and Mystic Shelter (41VV612).

MOTIF C. The third motif is present at all five sites. This motif contains anthropomorphs holding stafflike objects with enlarged distal ends.

PATTERNED DISTRIBUTION OF PICTOGRAPHIC ELEMENTS

I identified two significant patterns in the geographic distribution of pictographic elements—feathered hipclusters and winged figures associated with rabbit-eared anthropomorphs. Anthropomorphs with feathered hipclusters are present only at Panther Cave (41VV83). Although none of the other analyzed panels contained anthropomorphs with feather hipclusters, other sites within Seminole Canyon, such as Fate Bell Shelter (41VV74), contain this element. An anthropomorph with a feather hipcluster has also been identified at Hanging Cave (41VV79) located in Painted Canyon, less than two kilometers east of Panther Cave (fig. 3.11).

Winged and rabbit-eared anthropomorphs also have an identifiable distribution. These two elements occur together at Rattlesnake Canyon (41VV180) and are quite numerous—twenty-one winged anthropomorphs and seventeen anthropomorphs with rabbit ears. One winged anthropomorph was identified at

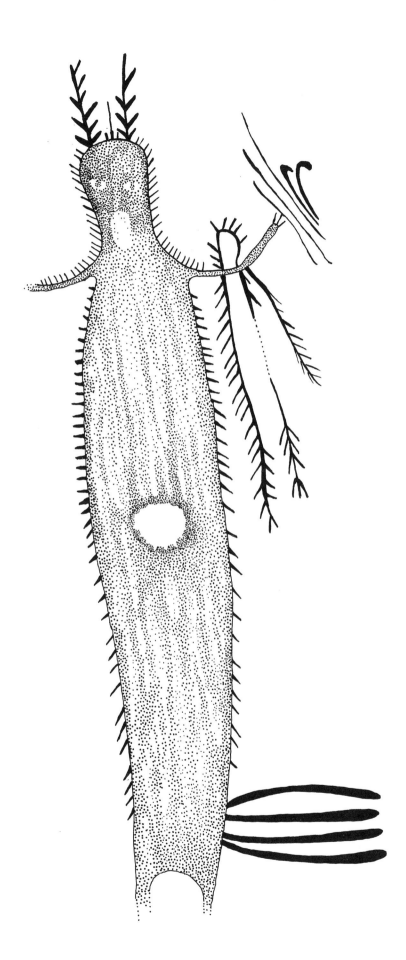

FIG. 3.11 Hanging Cave (41vv79).
Anthropomorph with
feather hipcluster.
Scale 1cm ≈ 8cm.

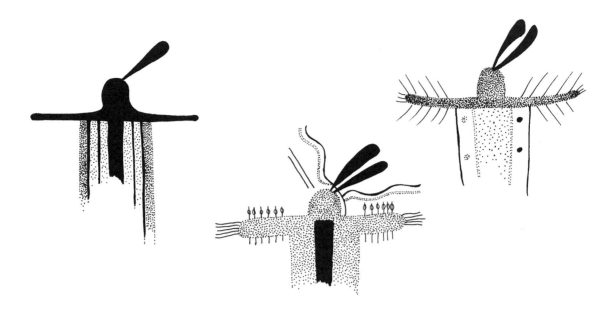

FIG. 3.12   Rabbit-eared anthropomorphs located in the vicinity of Painted Canyon west of the Pecos River. Sites 41VV584 *(left),* 41VV595 *(center),* and 41VV943 *(right).*

Cedar Springs (41VV696) and one at Panther Cave (41VV83). Northeast of Rattlesnake Canyon, however, several sites west of the Pecos River contained rabbit-eared anthropomorphs similar to the ones at Rattlesnake Canyon, including Eagle Cave (41VV167), approximately eight kilometers northeast of Rattlesnake Canyon, and sites 41VV576, 41VV584, 41VV595, and 41VV943 approximately twelve kilometers east of the canyon (fig. 3.12).

The geographic distribution of these pictographic elements suggests that they may be affiliated with specific clans or may be territorial markers; however, there are insufficient data at this time to adequately address these issues. A thorough survey of the rock art throughout the lower Pecos River region will be conducted in the future to determine the distribution of these elements across the landscape.

Four

GATEWAY SERPENTS AND OTHERWORLD JOURNEYS

Now the serpent was more crafty than any of the wild animals the Lord God had made.
He said to the woman, "Did God really say, 'You must not eat fruit from any tree in the garden?'"
The woman said to the serpent, "We may eat fruit from the trees in the garden,
but God did say, 'You must not eat from the tree that is in the middle of the garden,
and you must not touch it, or you will die.'"

"You will not surely die," the serpent said to the woman. "For God knows that when
you eat of it your eyes will be opened, and you will be like God, knowing good and evil."

GENESIS 3:1–5 New International Version

The pictographic elements of Motif A include a crenelated arch, an opening at the center of the arch, and a skeletonized anthropomorphic figure located above, below, or behind the arch. The anthropomorphs are either associated with a particular animal or their bodies have been adorned with animal attributes. My analysis involves a three-step approach: (1) to describe the motif identified at each site in the study; (2) to formulate a hypothesis regarding possible relationships between the motif and specific beliefs associated with the shamanic journey to the otherworld identified in ethnographic literature; and (3) to test the hypothesis against evidence from cognitive neuroscience research and the archaeological record.

Arches, Anthropomorphs, and Animals: A Pictographic Motif

The rock art panel located within Rattlesnake Canyon (41vv180) contains at least three

occurrences of Motif A. The first, found near the far left end of the panel depicts a centrastyled, rabbit-eared, red and black anthropomorphic figure superimposed over the top of a polychrome crenelated arch (fig. 4.1). A hole is painted in the top of the arch with red, yellow, and black lines radiating downward from this opening. The second appearance of this motif (see fig. 3.4) is found just to the right of the first figure. It is also a skeletonized, rabbit-eared, red and black anthropomorph. The object associated with the left hand of the anthropomorph has been identified as a spear-thrower, or atlatl (Kelley 1950, 1971). A staff-like object with an enlarged distal end is associated with the right hand. A circle, situated at the top of the crenelated arch, is painted over the chest area of the anthropomorphic figure. Above the anthropomorph are two red and black feline figures. The third occurrence of Motif A (fig. 4.2) is located to the lower right of the second figure. It includes a centrastyled, winged anthropomorph painted beneath a

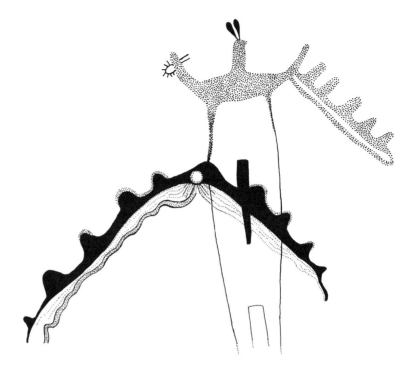

Rattlesnake Canyon (41VV180). Rabbit-eared, centrastyled anthropomorph painted over the top of a crenelated arch. Scale 1cm ≈ 18cm.

Rattlesnake Canyon (41VV180). Winged, centrastyled anthropomorph located beneath a crenelated arch. Scale 1cm ≈ 13cm.

crenelated arch. An opening at the top of the arch has lines radiating from the center outward.

The panel at the White Shaman site (41VV124) contains only one occurrence of Motif A (fig. 4.3). It depicts an elaborate

crenelated arch at the far left end of the panel. Unlike at Rattlesnake Canyon, however, the opening in the arch is not marked by a hole; instead, parallel lines run from the base of the arch through the top. Superimposed over the arch within the parallel lines is an antlered,

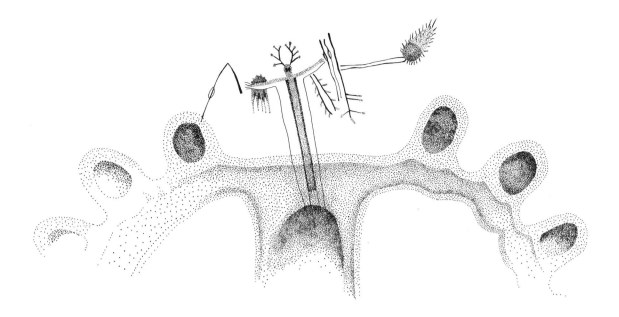

FIG.4.3   White Shaman (41vv124). Centrastyled, antlered anthropomorph passing through a crenelated arch. Scale 1cm ≈ 12cm.

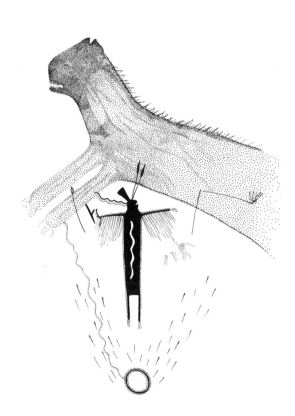

FIG.4.4   Panther Cave (41vv83). Winged, centrastyled anthropomorph associated with a crenelated line and a feline. Scale 1cm ≈ 30cm.

centrastyled anthropomorphic figure. This antlered anthropomorph is painted in red and dark gray, with lines running vertically down the center of the figure. Small black dots occur on the ends of the antler tines of the headdress. An atlatl is associated with the right hand of the anthropomorph; a stafflike object similar to that identified at Rattlesnake Canyon is associated with the left hand.

At least one, and perhaps two, occurrences of Motif A have been documented at Panther Cave (41vv83). One of the images is very difficult to discern due to overpainting and spalling damage (see fig. 3.6). The second image is found at the far right of the panel just beneath the large feline figure for which the site was named. A crenelated line is connected to a circle, from which many fine lines radiate out and upward. Just above the circle and below the feline is a winged, centrastyled anthropomorph with a bird-shaped head. Protruding from the head are two feathered darts and a possible feather headdress (fig. 4.4).

A vivid illustration of this recurring motif is located just left of center in the Mystic Shelter (41vv612) panel (fig. 4.5). It depicts a crenelated arch with an opening at the top.

FIG. 4.5   Mystic Shelter (41vv612). Centrastyled anthropomorph passing through an opening in a crenelated arch. Scale 1cm ≈ 14cm.

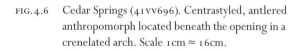

FIG. 4.6   Cedar Springs (41vv696). Centrastyled, antlered anthropomorph located beneath the opening in a crenelated arch. Scale 1cm ≈ 16cm.

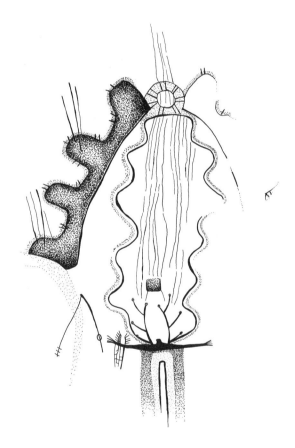

Superimposed over the opening and continuing on above it is a centrastyled anthropomorphic figure. This polychrome anthropomorph is painted in two shades of reddish brown pigment, fringed along both sides, with a sinuous black line running down the center of the figure. An atlatl is associated with the right hand and dart points with the left. Beneath the arch is a row of small black anthropomorphs surrounded by black and red dots. Beneath these anthropomorphs are several horizontal red and black lines.

Cedar Springs (41vv696) contains a clear example of Motif A (fig. 4.6). Located toward the right end of the panel is a crenelated arch with an elaborately painted opening at the top. The left side of the arch is painted black; the right side is white. Beneath the arch is an antlered, centrastyled anthropomorphic figure. Black dots adorn the ends of each antler tine.

Serpents, Shamans, and Spirit Companions: An Ethnographic Motif

My review of ethnographic literature revealed a recurring theme in the myths and folklore of cultures around the world that is similar to the pictographic motif described above (Boyd 1996). This motif is associated with beliefs about the journey taken by shamans to the spiritual realm.

The elements of the ethnographic motif include: (1) a universe that consists of various layers, with a supernatural realm below the earth's surface; (2) a serpent that serves as the gateway through which one must pass on the journey to the spirit world; (3) sacred portals or passageways, both natural and human made, that access the supernatural realm; and (4) the presence of animal spirit helpers or familiars.

KEY FEATURES OF SHAMANISM AND THE SHAMANIC JOURNEY

Dobkin de Rios and Winkleman (1989) noted that there is a lack of coherence in the use of the terms "shaman" and "shamanism." Mistakenly, the term "shaman" has been used to refer to a wide variety of trance practitioners, such as sorcerers, witches, prophets, seers, and diviners. Hultkrantz (1968) provided a clear definition for shamanism, one that has since been empirically supported through a cross-

cultural assessment of magico-religious practice in forty-seven societies. The fundamental elements of shamanism are as follows (Winkleman 1992): the shaman (1) establishes contact with the supernatural realm; (2) is the intermediary between the supernatural and members of his or her group; (3) receives inspiration from guardian or helping spirits that most commonly appear in the form of animals; (4) has ecstatic experiences that involve being able to enter an altered state of consciousness.

The concept of the universe consisting of various layers or cosmic regions is a belief common to many cultures around the world (Dupre 1975; Eliade 1964; Hultkrantz 1968; Katz, Biesele, and St. Denis 1997; Tooker 1979; Tylor 1970). For people who hold this view of their universe, the center, or *axis mundi,* is the point of intersection between these regions where communication with the spirit world is possible (Eliade 1959, 1964). This central axis passes through an opening or portal in the center of each region that gods and ancestors use to travel between the natural and supernatural realms. Through this opening the shaman's soul is able to enter the otherworld and personally confront supernatural forces, while serving as guardian of both the physical and psychic equilibrium of the group (Eliade 1959, 1964; Hultkrantz 1968; Winkleman 1986, 1992).

Certain geographic features, such as caves, mountains, and bodies of water, are frequently associated with the *axis mundi*. During shamanic initiations, caves are of particular importance and function as concrete symbols for passageways to another world or descent to the underworld. Eliade describes the initiation of the Smith Sound Eskimo as follows: "The aspirant must go at night to a cliff containing caves and walk straight ahead in the darkness. If he is destined to become a shaman, he will enter a cave; . . . [a]s soon as he has entered the cave, it closes behind him and does not open again until sometime later" (Eliade

1964:51). Caves are also of primary importance in North and South American shamanism as the location where aspirants have their dreams and meet their helping spirits (Eliade 1964).

A shaman gains access to the otherworld by entering an altered state of consciousness through such methods as the use of hallucinogenic plants, fasting, bloodletting, and self-hypnosis. When shamans enter an altered state, it is believed they have experienced "death." This death allows the soul of the shaman to leave the body and journey into the world beyond (Eliade 1959, 1964; Furst 1972, 1976; Winkleman 1992). The shaman's tutelary animal plays an important role as a guide and source of power during the shamanic journey into the otherworld, enabling the shaman to forsake the human condition. In mythical times, separation of humankind and the animal world had not yet occurred; this togetherness is reestablished each time the shaman merges with his or her animal spirit companion. The shaman experiences a ritual death, dying to this world and being reborn into the otherworld (Eliade 1964; Hultkrantz 1968).

The death and rebirth experience often involves either a mysterious illness or a symbolic ritual death that can involve dismemberment of the body, renewal of the organs, or being "killed" with arrows. This initiation involves an operation conducted by semidivine beings or an ancestor, whereby the body of the shaman is dismembered and internal organs and bones are replaced (Eliade 1964; Kalweit 1988). Before the "mystical organs" can be obtained, however, the shaman must gain the ability to see himself as a skeleton. According to Eliade, "To reduce oneself to the skeleton condition is equivalent to reentering the womb of this primordial life, that is, to a complete renewal, a mystical rebirth" (Eliade 1964:63).

SHAMANIC IDEOLOGIES OF MESOAMERICA AND THE AMERICAN SOUTHWEST

Shamanic ideology is entrenched in the mythology and folklore of numerous cultures in Mesoamerica and the American Southwest, including Aztec, Huichol, Yaqui, and Hopi. It is especially identifiable in those societies concerned with life after death and shamanic journeys to the otherworld.

AZTECS. The Aztecs—whose ancestors were the wandering hunter-gatherer Chichimecs of the Chihuahuan desert—perceived their cosmos as divided into several vertically aligned horizontal layers. The world above the earth consisted of thirteen layers of heavens; below the earth were the nine layers of Mictlan, the land of the dead. Entrance into Mictlan was obtained through a cave conceived as the gaping jaws of a reptilian earth monster (Brundage 1979; Ortiz de Montellano 1990; Pasztory 1983).

Caves, or *oztotl,* as defined in the Florentine Codex, were the place of the dead: "Our mothers, our fathers have gone to rest in the water, in the cave, the place of no openings, the place of no smoke hole, the place of the dead" (Sahagún 1963:277). Caves were also magical places that provided access to the world of the supernatural: "It is wide-mouthed; it is narrow-mouthed. It has mouths which pass through to the other side. I place myself in the cave. I enter the cave" (Dibble and Anderson 1970:276). Burial in natural and artificial caves was common among the Aztecs (Heyden 1981). Replicas of caves were created to serve as portals to the land of the dead. For example, in Book 3 of the Florentine Codex, Sahagún (1978) discussed the cremation process for the bodies of Aztec noblemen and commoners. He noted that after cremation was complete, the Aztecs "dug a round hole in which to place it (cremated ashes): a pit. This they called a cave" (Sahagún 1978:45).

Another example of the replication of sacred geography is illustrated in Aztec architecture. The ruins of many Aztec sites contain structures known as ballcourts, or *tlachco*. In the exact center of the ballcourt is a circular flagstone that represents the cosmic center, the *axis mundi*. In Aztec mythology Quetzalcoatl, the feathered serpent, was said to have opened this sacred portal into the world below (Brundage 1979:11). Aztec art depicts the prominent role of the serpent in Aztec cosmology. According to Pasztory, "The most elaborate animal structures are feathered serpents with an earth monster carved under the base. They signify the green surface of the earth overlying the voracious underworld" (1983:234). The concept of a serpent as the earth's surface covering the world below is illustrated in the Codex Selden Roll (fig. 4.7). This codex contains a depiction of the cave birthplace, Chicomoztoc. The mouth of the cave is symbolized by the maw of the earth monster. Covering the maw is a serpentine arch that represents the earth's surface.

The serpent representing the earth's surface is also illustrated in an Aztec stone sculpture from Tenochtitlán dating to around the turn of the sixteenth century. This sculpture, which is displayed at the Museo Nacional de Antropología in Mexico City, depicts a coiled, feathered serpent with a face emerging from its open jaws. Underneath the serpent stone is a relief of the earth monster. Pasztory (1983: 162) stated that "the human face emerging from the maw of a feathered serpent probably renders an image of rebirth. In Mesoamerican art the disappearance and reappearance of the sun, the stars, and the planets were represented metaphorically as being swallowed and regurgitated by a monster which often demonstrated serpent characteristics."

Other animals also had supernatural associations. Ortiz de Montellano (1990:67) stated that Aztec religion combined "an elaborate

FIG. 4.7   Codex Selden Roll. The open maw of the earth monster as depicted in Aztec codices.
Redrawn from Heyden (1981).

state religion with shamanism." Human-animal transformation and animal spirit helpers were among the characteristics in Aztec religion that were associated with shamanism. Aztecs believed the animistic force of a shaman, *tonalli,* could enter the shaman's animal double, *nahualli.* Aztec gods were also believed to transform at will into their animal familiars (Ortiz de Montellano 1990). According to Brundage (1979:82), the ancient Chichimec god known to the Aztecs as Tezcatlipoca excelled beyond all other Aztec gods at transforming into his animal familiar, the jaguar. Brundage credits this well-established ability to transform into an animal to Tezcatlipoca's shamanic origins (Brundage 1979:82).

HUICHOL. The Huichol live in the highland geographic zone of the Sierra Madre Occidentals in the states of Jalisco and Nayarit in northwestern Mexico. According to Huichol tradition, their nomadic hunting-and-gathering Chichimec ancestors migrated into the area from a northern ancestral homeland in the Chihuahuan Desert (Myerhoff 1974; Schaefer and Furst 1996).

The Huichol perceive the world as surrounded by the sea, which with its snakelike motions is the largest of all serpents. A two-headed serpent serves as a gateway through which the sun must pass upon setting each day on its journey to the world below (Lumholtz 1900, 1902; Myerhoff 1974). The concept of the serpent as the gateway to the world below is demonstrated in Huichol myth and art.

A hole made in the center of the Huichol ceremonial temple floor serves as their *axis mundi,* allowing communication with the supernatural realm. This sacred cavity is believed to be the doorway through which the shaman descends on his magical flight into the otherworld (Myerhoff 1974; Zingg 1977). Covering this sacred cavity is a small stone disk referred to as a god disk (Lumholtz 1900; Myerhoff 1974). In Huichol mythology, it was

otuanaka, the Corn Mother, who commanded that the sacred hole be covered with a god disk and that the disk be engraved with her animals: snakes of blue, green, and yellow (Zingg 1977).

In a yarn painting created by José Benítez Sánchez, a Huichol shaman/artist, the soul of the deceased is depicted journeying to the land of the dead (fig. 4.8). The destination of the soul lies through a serpentine arch at the base of the painting. The small, upside-down, centrastyled anthropomorphic figure with a vertical band running down the center of the body represents the shaman. According to the Huichol shaman/artist Ramon Medina, the practice of depicting the shaman in this skeletonized fashion is done specifically so that the figure is recognized as a shaman. When asked why it is done that way, Ramon responded, "Because that is how it was established in the time of the ancestors" (Furst 1978:23).

The Huichol soul, being guided by the shaman in the middle of the painting, is depicted passing through the passageway that leads to the world below. The land of the dead is illustrated at the base of the painting by a serpentine arch, possibly representing the serpent that surrounds the world, which divides the land of the dead from the land of the living. Other animals are also associated with the supernatural. Among the Huichol, the deer is a sacred and magical animal. Kauyumári, also known as Sacred Deer Person, is the anthropomorphized tutelary animal of the Huichol shaman. One of Kauyumári's most important services is to act as intermediary between the shaman and the gods. According to Myerhoff (1974:85), there is reason to believe that Kauyumári is "closely modeled on an actual historical personage, perhaps an important early *mara'akame* (shaman) who later merged with the Sacred Deer Person." Kauyumári is conceived both in the form of a deer and as a person wearing antlers (Furst 1972; Schaefer and Furst 1996).

FIG. 4.8 Huichol yarn painting, *Journey of the Soul.* Yarn painting by José Benítez Sánchez illustrating a Huichol soul journeying to the land of the dead. Redrawn from Berrin (1978).

YAQUI. Prior to Spanish contact, Yaqui Indians were dispersed throughout the state of Sonora in northwestern Mexico. Today, Yaqui settlements are located in southern Arizona, California, and elsewhere in the western United States (Spicer 1940). As with the Aztec and the Huichol, accessing the otherworld is a prominent part of Yaqui mythology.

The Yaqui homeland and way of life— *yoania*—and the beliefs associated with them form the basis of Yaqui thought and character (Painter 1986:3). The Surem, which the Yaqui believe to be their ancestors, lived a nomadic life in a world where nature and man had a common psychic life, communicating through a gift called *seataka.* This was the way things were before the prophecy given through the Talking Tree (Painter 1986; Spicer 1940). In the legend of the Talking Tree, a vibrating tree, or stick, foretells the coming of Christianity. Those who were willing to accept this new way of life continued to live as Yaquis in Yaqui country. Those who were unwilling to accept the changes went underground as

Surem, taking the *yoania* with them. The Yaqui believe the *yoania* and the Surem are still there today. Their secrets can be learned through *yoania* visions, which can appear in far-off places such as secret mountain caves or be communicated through dreams (Painter 1986).

Only those individuals who possess the gift of *seataka,* who are earnest in their desire to seek the *yoania,* and who are courageous enough to endure the frightening trials associated with obtaining *yoania* visions are successful in learning the Surem secrets. This terrifying ordeal involves an encounter with a huge snake. Entrance and exit to the supernatural world of *yoania* must be made through the mouth of a giant serpent (Painter 1986). This portal to the otherworld was noted by Beals (1943) in his study *The Aboriginal Culture of the Cahita Indians,* which included the Uto-Aztecan-speaking Yaqui and Mayo. He noted that "despite the documentary statement that shamans inherited office, often they acquired power through visions, possibly through dreams, or through some form of initiation which involved death-and-resurrection concepts that included being swallowed and passed through the body of a snake dwelling in a cave" (Beals 1943:64). The source of a shaman's power, according to Beals, "was the dream or vision, through which an individual acquired the assistance of a spirit, in animal form usually, which helped him or over which he had certain control" (Beals 1943:64).

The *pascola* dance group is frequently mentioned in association with *yoania* visions. *Pascola* dances are kept separate from church-sponsored activities and are performed as the result of a *yoania* vision obtained in a dream. The Yaqui maintain that *pascola* knowledge comes from the animals of *yoania* rather than from Christian supernaturals. *Pascola* rituals and music are thought to have originally come "from a snake which lived in the water in the mountains" (Spicer 1940:261).

HOPI. The Hopi of northern Arizona believe the universe consists of various cosmic levels. The world below is conceived of as a series of waterways beneath the earth. The horned water serpent, residing in the interior of the earth, is overseer of this watery world and over all the waters of the earth. For the Hopi, the serpent serves as the communicator between the earthly world and the world below. Snakes are released after ceremonies to carry messages to the spirits residing in these watery depths (H. Tyler 1964).

The Hopi also believe several other animals possess supernatural power. These tutelary animals or spirit companions enable magico-religious practitioners, such as shamans and witches, to forsake their human condition in order to gain power from the supernatural realm. Transformation into animals and obtaining power from animals is "a concept rendered collective through the [Pueblo] societies" (Parsons 1974:63). The transformation is "effected through putting on the animal pelt

or through turning over, that is passing through a hoop or ring" (Parsons 1974:66n).

In Hopi cosmology, caves are revered as openings to the world below where the serpent and other supernaturals reside. These openings are symbolized by a hole, called a *sipapu,* that is made in the center of the ceremonial kiva floor. The *sipapu* is kept sealed except during ceremonies, when it serves as a symbolic entrance into the world below (Ortiz 1972; Waters 1963).

Otherworld Journeys of the Lower Pecos Archaic

My review of the literature revealed striking similarities between the iconographic expression and ideology associated with the shamanic journey among indigenous peoples of Mesoamerica and the American Southwest, and the Pecos River–style pictographs of the lower Pecos region (Boyd 1996). Four common elements identified in Aztec, Huichol, Yaqui, and Hopi worldview and cosmology provide a possible explanation for the lower Pecos rock art motif. These four elements are (1) a multilayered universe, with a supernatural realm below the earth's surface; (2) a serpent as the gateway to the spirit world; (3) sacred portals or passageways to access the supernatural realm; and (4) animal spirit helpers or familiars. I believe the elements of the pictographic motif are graphic representations of shamanic journeys from this world to the otherworld.

Each of these four Uto-Aztecan groups has similar cosmological beliefs and ideologies associated with the shamanic journey to the spirit or otherworld, which I use to explain Motif A. But I am not implying that the Archaic inhabitants of the region were necessarily Uto-Aztecan speakers. At this time, we do not know what language was spoken by the peoples living in the region during the Archaic period.

THE CRENELATED ARCH
AND THE SERPENT

The ethnographic examples describe a layered universe with a supernatural realm existing below the earth's surface. Each group shares the concept of the serpent as being either a barrier or gateway through which the shaman must pass to access this spiritual realm. The crenelated arch associated with Motif A in the lower Pecos rock art is analogous to the serpent as the barrier or gateway through which the shaman must pass on his or her journey to the otherworld. As in the Aztec ideology, it represents the earth's surface, which overlies the voracious and watery underworld, the land of the ancestors. This is most clearly illustrated at Mystic Shelter (see fig. 4.5). At the base of the crenelated arch is a horizontal band of red and black lines that may represent the rivers of the underworld. The small anthropomorphic figures contained within the arch could represent the ancestors or spirit beings that reside in the land of the dead. In some societies the spirits of the dead are the shaman's helpers. During healing ceremonies, the shaman sends the spirits of the dead to find and retrieve the strayed soul of the ailing person (Eliade 1964).

THE PORTAL TO THE
OTHERWORLD

The concept of sacred portals or passageways, both natural and human made, through which the shaman can access the supernatural realm is a common element in belief systems of many groups in Mesoamerica and the American Southwest. The opening in the crenelated arch is analogous to this portal or *axis mundi*. In the natural landscape, caves, rockshelters, sinkholes, and other "holes" in the earth's surface—the serpent's body—serve as portals to the otherworld. Although crenelated arches and crenelated lines are a common motif in the Pecos River–style pictographs, not all have openings in the crenelation. When they do, they are usually associated with skeletonized anthropomorphs.

SKELETONIZATION,
ANIMALS, AND SHAMANIC
TRANSFORMATION

In the belief systems of the cultural groups discussed, the shaman must experience a ritual death in order to be reborn into the spiritual realm. This ritual death and rebirth involves the merging of the shaman and an animal familiar. In the lower Pecos rock art, the skeletonized anthropomorphic figures located above, below, or behind a crenelated arch represent the shaman undertaking the journey to the otherworld. Skeletonization—the decoration of the central portion of the figure—is used by indigenous artists around the world to illustrate death and resurrection. As Eliade stated, "the reduction to the skeleton indicates a passing beyond the profane human condition and, hence, a deliverance from it. . . . To reduce oneself to a skeleton condition is equivalent to re-entering the womb of this primordial life, that is, to a complete renewal, a mystical rebirth" (Eliade 1964:63). As indicated by the Huichol shaman, the practice of depicting the shaman in the skeletonized fashion is done specifically so that the figure will be recognized as that of a shaman (Furst 1978:23).

The animals and animal attributes associated with these skeletonized figures represent the shaman's animal familiar or helping spirits, which are of central importance in the death and rebirth of the shaman. According to Eliade: "The presence of a helping spirit in animal form, dialog with it in a secret language, or incarnation of such an animal spirit by the shaman (masks, actions, dances, etc.) is another way of showing that the shaman can forsake his human condition, is able, in a word, to 'die.' From the most distant times almost all animals have been conceived of as psychopomps that accompany the soul into the beyond or as the dead person's new form. Whether it is the 'ancestor' or the 'initiatory master,' *the animal symbolizes a real and direct connection with the beyond*" (Eliade 1964:93; emphasis added). At each of the analyzed sites, the skeletonized anthropomorphs— shamans—are either surrounded by their animal familiars or have been transformed into them.

Neuroscience, Shamanism, and Rock Art Imagery

Ethnographic literature provides only one strand of evidence in the cablelike argument I propose. As stated by R. L. Kelly (1995:339), "the translation of information from ethnography to archaeology cannot be direct." Therefore, I test the shamanic journey hypothesis formulated through ethnographic analogy against evidence from cognitive neuroscience and the archaeological record.

COGNITIVE NEUROSCIENCE AND ALTERED STATES OF CONSCIOUSNESS

The crux of shamanic practice is the acquisition of supernatural power through the technique of trance. Trance research conducted within the cognitive neurosciences has illuminated the relevance of mental imagery, somatic hallucinations, and the emotional effects of altered states of consciousness to rock art production (Blackburn 1977; Hedges 1976, 1983, 1994; Lewis-Williams and Dowson 1988; Whitley 1999).

BIOLOGY OF TRANCE. The trance state is a measurable biological phenomenon. The shamanic journey—passage from the physical realm to the spiritual realm—occurs when a shaman deliberately induces trance through such methods as auditory driving (rhythmic drumming and chanting), fasting and thirsting, sleep deprivation, self-hypnosis, or the ingestion of hallucinogenic drugs. By examining the trance state, cognitive neuroscience provides insight into neurological processes associated with shamanic travel between the two realms. Brain-imaging studies of neurological activity in individuals during trance show significant decreased activity in the posterior superior parietal lobe. This region of the brain has been identified as the orientation association area, or OAA (Newberg, D'Aquili, and Rause 2001). The OAA helps to regulate our sense of self by orienting an individual spatially, allowing us to negotiate the physical landscape. To perform these crucial functions, the OAA "must draw a sharp distinction between the individual and everything else, to sort out the you from the infinite not-you that makes up the rest of the universe" (Newberg, D'Aquili, and Rause 2001:5). During trance, there is a sharp reduction in activity in the OAA, triggering the very real perception that the self is endless and interwoven with the universe. As humans, throughout time and across the globe, we are all capable of experiencing this sensation. Our interpretation of the experience, however, is largely dictated by our culture. One of the most expressive and effective means of communicating this trance experience has been and continues to be through art—the production of visionary images (Irwin 1994; Reichel-Dolmatoff 1978a).

ENTOPTIC PHENOMENA. Individuals entering a trance state experience a well-defined range of luminous visual percepts that are caused by an excitation of the central nervous system. These visual percepts are very much alike from one person to another, repeatedly appearing as geometric forms, such as grids, wavy lines, circles, spirals, and crosses. They are experienced as shimmering, moving, rotating patterns that grade one into the other, combining in a multitude of ways. Because these visual percepts derive from the central nervous system, all people entering an altered state of consciousness are likely to experience them, no matter what their cultural background (Horowitz 1964, 1975; Klüver 1926, 1942, 1966; Siegel 1977, 1984; C. Tyler 1978).

The geometric images associated with altered states of consciousness are referred to variously in the medical literature as phosphenes, form constants, and entoptic phenomena. In fact, they have different biological origins. Phosphenes are sensations perceived by the human brain as visual images in the absence of visual stimuli; they are entophthalmic—within the eye—and can be produced by physical stimulation, such as placing pressure on the eyeball (Oster 1970). Form constants derive deep in the visual pathway, most likely beyond the eye in the cortex itself (Siegel 1977). C. Tyler (1978:1633) defined entoptic phenomena as visual sensations derived from structures within the eye, as well as images originating elsewhere in the visual system. By Tyler's definition, entoptic phenomena include visual percepts categorized as phosphenes and form constants.

HALLUCINATIONS. Entoptics are not the same as hallucinations. A hallucination may be defined as a state whereby a subject experiences perceptual changes in his or her environment that appear to be inappropriate to an observer (Winters 1975). Unlike entoptics, hallucinations can occur in any sensory modality, visual, auditory, olfactory, gustatory, tactile, or kinesthetic. They may also be synesthetic—a subjective sensation or image of a sense other than the one being stimulated (La Barre 1975). For example, the beat of a drum may stimulate visual hallucinations or cause the kinesthetic hallucinatory experience

of being lifted into the air. Visual hallucinations differ from entoptic phenomena in that they include *culturally* controlled, complex, iconic imagery such as landscapes, people, animals, places, and objects, as opposed to entoptics that are universally experienced and include strictly geometric imagery.

COGNITIVE NEUROSCIENCE AND ROCK ART INTERPRETATION

Ethnography and medical science provide examples of visionary phenomena associated with trance or altered states of consciousness that can be used to validate shamanistic interpretations of rock art motifs around the world. In 1970 Gerald Oster observed that phosphene-like imagery appears in prehistoric cave paintings and in folk art from many cultures and different time periods. He stated that art historians "might well consider the possible effects of phosphenes as an 'intrinsic' source of inspiration for men of many different societies when they are speculating on relations and cross influences among primitive cultures" (1970:83). After Oster noted the similarities between entoptics and rock art imagery, researchers successfully constructed explanatory models that combine ethnography and cognitive neuroscience research to aid in the identification and interpretation of shamanic art (Blackburn 1977; Hedges 1982, 1994; Lewis-Williams and Dowson 1988; Reichel-Dolmatoff 1978a, 1978b; Turpin 1994; Whitley 1998, 1999).

One of the first rock art researchers to link ethnography and cognitive neuroscience was Thomas Blackburn (1977). Blackburn was inspired by the pioneering fieldwork of Colombian anthropologist Gerardo Reichel-Dolmatoff among the Tukano Indians of South America. Reichel-Dolmatoff (1978a) advanced a hypothesis that links certain forms of artistic expression with entoptic phenomena that are frequently encountered during hallucinatory experiences. Blackburn (1977) argued that the geometric design elements characteristic of the Chumash rock art in California were inspired by hallucinatory phenomena associated with the ingestion of *Datura inoxia*. He advanced the following hypotheses: artistic design motifs having a wide distribution around the world will tend to bear a striking and significant resemblance to phosphene images, and phosphene-based motifs will tend to be particularly common in art produced in connection with ritual usages of hallucinogenic drugs.

Concurrently, Ken Hedges began demonstrating the link between mental imagery and the rock art of southern California, Arizona, and other regions of the American Southwest. Hedges demonstrated that characteristic visionary phenomena and design motifs derived from dream and vision experiences support the interpretation of certain rock art motifs, compositions, and sites as direct portrayals of the visionary images of trance state, or as art styles derived from such images (Hedges 1976, 1982).

Lewis-Williams and Dowson (1988:201) developed a "neuropsychological model" that seeks to explain rock art imagery associated with the trance experience of shamans. This approach developed out of their research in South Africa, where the shamanic nature of the art, coupled with detailed ethnographic accounts of South African San trance rituals, directed their attention to altered states of consciousness and the cognitive neurosciences. Based on a review of laboratory studies of altered states of consciousness induced by hallucinogenic drugs, migraine headaches, and other means, Lewis-Williams and Dowson (1988) developed three components of the neuropsychological model: (1) entoptic forms associated with altered states; (2) principles governing the perception of entoptics; and (3) stages in the progression of altered states of consciousness. These three components link the rock art imagery to imagery associated with altered states and to ritual behavior.

The first component of the model identifies six geometric forms that appear as visual images during the initial stages of trance. These entoptic forms are grids or lattices, parallel lines, dots and short flecks, zigzags (both angular and undulating), concentric circles or nested U-shaped lines, and meandering lines. The second component presents the ways in which entoptics can be perceived during an altered state. Entoptic forms can be *replicated* (appearing in one of the fundamental forms), *fragmented* (broken down into minimal components), *integrated* with other imagery, *superimposed* over other entoptic forms, *juxtaposed* next to other entoptics, *reduplicated* or multiples of a form, and *rotated*. The third component involves identifying three stages in the development of mental imagery. In stage 1—the initial stage of an altered state—individuals experience entoptic forms (not an iconic hallucination). Entoptics can be perceived with the eyes open or closed and are not consciously controlled. These are often characterized by a variety of saturated colors. As individuals progress into a deeper trance state and enter stage 2, they try to makes sense of the entoptic images, to decode or recognize forms. They will use similes to describe the experience; for example, indicating that the grid pattern "looks like a honeycomb" or the undulating lines "look like a snake." In stage 3—the deepest stage of trance—the entoptics are elaborated into iconic images or what might be described as a "full-blown" hallucination. As individuals lose the ability to discriminate between literal and analogous meanings, similes are no longer used to describe the forms. The iconic images are often projected against a background of geometric forms. Here, metaphor overcomes simile; no longer do the wavy lines look like snakes; they *are* snakes.

COGNITIVE NEUROSCIENCE AND THE OTHERWORLD JOURNEY MOTIF

Reichel-Dolmatoff (1978a) conducted a study of hallucinatory imagery experienced by the Tukano Indians in the Colombian northwest Amazon. In his study, he asked Tukano shamans to draw pictures of the visions they experienced while under the influence of the hallucinogenic *yagé*. The complex geometric images drawn by the shaman were the same geometric patterns that were used in pictographs and petroglyphs, and that decorated their vessels, pottery, baskets, bodies, and buildings. They were also the same geometric forms identified in research about altered states and later used by researchers to explain rock art imagery around the world (Blackburn 1977; Hedges 1976, 1994; Lewis-Williams and Dowson 1988; Whitley 1988, 1998). These entoptic forms are present in the pictographs of the lower Pecos, including the recurring otherworld journey motif. This motif has many elements that are plainly referable to sensations and images experienced in the trance state.

SERPENTS IN THE MIND. A common entoptic form associated with altered states is zigzag or undulating lines that cross the field of vision. This visual percept is similar to the crenelated lines that form the arch of the motif. Illusions associated with the ingestion of mescaline (Maclay and Guttman 1941; Siegel and Jarvik 1975) and with migraine hallucinations (Richards 1971) are very similar to the motif. These illusions have been described by Richards (1971:89): "It generally begins near the center of the visual field as a small, gray area with indefinite boundaries. . . . During the next few minutes the gray area slowly expands into a horseshoe, with bright zigzag lines appearing at the outer edge. These lines are small at first and grow as the blind

area expands and moves outward toward the periphery of the visual field."

Individuals who enter an altered state of consciousness frequently describe the undulating lines as snakes (Horowitz 1964). One of the forms repeated in the Tukano vision drawings elicited by Reichel-Dolmatoff is that of crenelated lines, which according to the Tukano, represent either the Snake Canoe of their creation myth or *yagé* snakes (Reichel-Dolmatoff 1978a). Harner (1973a), Dobkin de Rios (1973) and Narby (1998) listed large, brightly colored snakes as first among the most frequently reported images experienced by Peruvian *ayahuasceros* in an altered state.

Often the individual reports two snakes or the sensation of being surrounded by snakes. This may be due to "bilateral duplication" or "reduplication," redundant elements of simple forms in hallucinatory and pseudohallucinatory images (Horowitz 1975:179). "Deep hallucinations submerged me. I suddenly found myself surrounded by two gigantic boa constrictors that seemed fifty feet long. . . . My eyes are closed and I see a spectacular world of brilliant lights, and in the middle of these hazy thoughts, the snakes start talking to me without words" (Narby 1998:7). Schaefer (Schaefer and Furst 1996) received various descriptions from Huichol consultants of snake imagery associated with peyote-induced visions. A Huichol woman reported: "I saw some animals that looked like snakes of many colors, some were striped. They filled the room. I turned and saw up above it was filled with snakes. Wherever I turned there were snakes all over" (Schaefer and Furst 1996: 156). Peyote-induced tactile hallucinations involving snakes were also reported by one of Schaefer's consultants, who reported feeling snakes slither across and curl around his body (Schaefer and Furst 1996:159).

A LIGHT AT THE END OF THE TUNNEL. The opening in the arch, which is pictographically represented as either a circle or as parallel lines, can also be explained in terms of imagery associated with stage 3. During this final stage in the development of mental imagery, individuals report a vortex or tunnel-like image surrounding and engulfing them. At the end of the tunnel is a very bright light or hole. The bright light in the center of the field of vision obscures details but allows images on the periphery to be observed. Siegel (1977) stated that the location of this point of light creates the tunnel-like perspective. The surrounding images pulsate, moving toward the center of the tunnel or away from the light, sometimes moving in both directions. This experience was described by one individual as follows: "It's sort of like a tube, like I sort of feel—like sort of—that I'm at the bottom of a tube looking up. You can see the slides (imagery) converging with a point in the center" (Siegel 1977:134).

Individuals report feeling as though they are falling into this vortex or flying through the tunnel at incredible rates of speed. Geometric forms begin combining, duplicating, and superimposing; then they are replaced by complex imagery, including recognizable scenes, people, and objects. At this point that they have crossed over to the otherworld (Siegel 1992). "The mouth of the tunnel turned toward me as it writhed and pulsated, a Euclidian snake pregnant with light and form. Suddenly it disgorged a storm of images, stars, pinwheels, snowflakes, mosaics, and fans" (Siegel 1992:15).

I believe the opening in the crenelated arch in lower Pecos iconography represents a portal—the *axis mundi*—through which the shaman could access the spiritual realm. Trance research provides support for this explanation. The opening in the arch, which is frequently illustrated with yellow, orange, or red lines emanating from it, represents the bright light at the end of the tunnel experienced during an altered state. The arch is

formed by the bilateral duplication of one of the recurring visual percepts—undulating lines. The addition of the circle or parallel lines running down the center of the arch forms a conical shape, the shape of the funnel or tube that is also a recurrent element in altered states.

I HAVE WINGS! Each of the anthropomorphs in the otherworld journey motif is associated with an animal or is adorned with the attributes of a particular animal. This aspect of the motif has been explained as the union of the shaman with his or her animal familiar, a vitally important component of the shamanic journey to the otherworld. The feeling of transformation from human to animal can, as with the crenelated arch and portal, be explained in terms of cognitive neuroscience.

Mental imagery is but one of the experiences associated with an altered state. Individuals also report auditory, olfactory, gustatory, kinesthetic, tactile, and synesthetic hallucinations. Tactile hallucinations often lead individuals to believe they are turning into animals. These hallucinations, which usually begin as itching skin on the hands, legs, and back, give the sensation of growing hair or sprouting wings (Harner 1973b; Siegel and Jarvik 1975).

I thought of a fox, and instantly I was transformed into that animal. I could feel myself a fox, could see my long ears and bushy tail, and by a sort of introversion felt that my complete anatomy was that of a fox. Suddenly, the point of vision changed. My eyes seemed to be located at the back of my mouth: I looked out between parted lips, saw the two rows of pointed teeth, and, closing my mouth with a snap, saw nothing. (Siegel and Jarvik 1975:104–105)

When I turn into a lion, I can feel my lion-hair growing and my teeth forming. I'm inside that lion, no longer a person. Others to whom I appear see me as just another lion. (Katz, Biesele, and St. Denis 1997:24)

I felt that it was no longer a hand but the tip of a wing, I was turning into a winged being. I then stretched my wings and felt extreme freedom and expansion. My wings were growing. . . . I have wings! I have wings! (Naranjo 1973:180)

The sensation of body dismemberment and alteration has also been reported by individuals in an altered state. The following description was reported by an individual experiencing henbane intoxication. Henbane is a European member of the nightshade family. "My feet were growing lighter, expanding and breaking loose from my body. Each part of my body seemed to be going off on its own. My head was growing independently larger, and I was seized with the fear that I was falling apart" (Harner 1973b:139). For millennia, shamans

taking the otherworld journey have visually documented those journeys. Many of the rock art panels in the lower Pecos provide us with a window into the trance experience.

SHAMANIC TRANSFORMATION IN THE LOWER PECOS ARCHAIC

Housed within Mystic Shelter is an especially vivid illustration of the coalescing of shaman and animal familiar. It contains all the elements identified as a part of the otherworld journey motif (fig. 4.9).

The Mystic Shelter panel contains a large feline figure, approximately three meters long, with red lines emanating from its nose and mouth. The head of this figure meets the tip of the tail of another feline. The tail, legs, and claws have been disarticulated from the body of this second figure. Due to water damage, it is not possible to determine whether the head

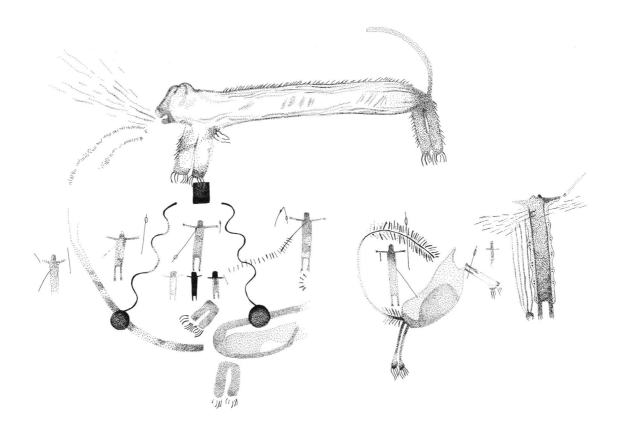

FIG. 4.9   Mystic Shelter (41vv612). Rock art imagery depicting the merger of human and animal. Scale 1 cm ≈ 28 cm.

of the feline was originally painted or not. In front of this figure is a headless feline with attached appendages. It is clear that the head was not originally painted. Note also the manner in which the legs and claws are illustrated in comparison to the previous felines. Instead of being thick and rigid, they are depicted as thin and limp.

Associated with the feline figures are five red, nonskeletonized, impaled anthropomorphs and one skeletonized figure. The first red anthropomorph appears just to the left of the feline with disarticulated appendages. The second appears to the left of a crenelated arch, and the third under the arch. Beneath the third figure is a row of three small yellow and black anthropomorphs. The fourth red anthropomorph is located to the right of the arch. The fifth is encircled by the tail of the headless feline. A line, probably a spear, runs from the rump of the feline and connects with this fifth anthropomorph. The fifth anthropomorph is not just red; it contains a red orange color similar to the color painted on the rump of the headless feline. In front of the headless feline is an ornate, headless skeletonized anthropomorph. A series of lines emanate from the headless feline and across the body of the headless anthropomorph.

The various components involved in the merger of shaman and animal are clearly illustrated in this section of the panel. The animal familiar is a feline, perhaps a mountain lion. It is depicted in three different forms, representing three different stages in the merger of human and animal. The shaman is depicted at least five times as a nonskeletonized anthropomorph prior to the transformation. Across the top of the panel, the first feline is painted so as to indicate action, a leaping position. The second feline is illustrated quite differently from the first. Its appendages are disarticulated— tail, legs, and claws are all separating from the body. This is very similar to the description

offered by the individual experiencing henbane intoxication, in which he felt his body falling apart. It is also similar to Eliade's discussion of shamanic initiation involving dismemberment, whereby the initiate receives "renewed organs and bones" from his or her helping spirit (1964:63).

The next feline, headless and with limp and lifeless limbs, is depicted at an approximate sixty degree angle, a posture common to individuals entering a trance state (Goodman, Henney, and Pressel 1974). The red lines emanating from the headless feline and crossing to the headless, skeletonized anthropomorph may represent the nose bleed associated with individuals entering trance (Eliade 1964; Lewis-Williams 1992), bloodletting (Schele and Miller 1986), or the blood of a dying animal.

As with the felines, each anthropomorphic figure in the Mystic Shelter panel illustrates a stage in the transformation. Each is impaled with a spear, representing the ritual symbolic killing of the shaman. The figure located between the two crenelated lines is not skeletonized, indicating that transformation is not complete. The three yellow and black figures located beneath the red anthropomorph represent helping spirits or ancestors that assist in the transformation. The merger of human and animal begins with the fifth anthropomorph. This is illustrated by the encircling of the figure with the tail of the feline, by the line connecting the two, and by the color passing from the rump of the feline, up the line, and into the anthropomorph. The headless, skeletonized anthropomorph represents the completed transformation. The shaman has contemplated his own skeleton, received the mystical organs and renewed bones, and experienced ritual death. The cycle is complete; the mythical time when animals and humans were not separated is reestablished and the journey to the otherworld begins.

Archaeology of the Otherworld

The archaeological record in the lower Pecos and surrounding regions provides an additional strand of evidence that can be used to support my explanation of the journey motif. A common burial method noted throughout the Chihuahuan Desert and adjacent lands, including the lower Pecos region, was to drop the body in a vertical shaft cave or sinkhole (Aveleyra, Maldonado, and Martinez 1956; Bement 1994; Turpin 1988). The deposits of Seminole Sink (41vv620) contained the remains of at least twenty-two individuals from the Early Archaic period. Although numerous other caves and rockshelters have produced interments, "Seminole Sink produced the first cemetery-like burial population in the region" (Bement 1989:67). Additional vertical shaft caves with human remains have been identified since the excavation of Seminole Sink in 1984 (Bement 1994).

Turpin (1988) provided possible explanations for the use of sinkholes as burial chambers in the lower Pecos. She suggested that burial of the dead in sinkholes might have been a response to the belief in "animas persisting in forms ranging from beneficial spirits to malevolent ghosts. . . . If the ghost is malevolent and seeks to torment the living, the sinkhole may have served as a sealed sepulcher to contain the spirits" (Turpin 1988:125). Other possible explanations offered by Turpin include returning the dead to the womb of Mother Earth, rapid disposal of the bodies and abandonment of the area, or simply a convenient location for "pedestrian pallbearers."

Based on ethnographic literature and the elements of the otherworld journey motif in lower Pecos art, disposal of the dead in sinkholes most likely involved ideas of death and regeneration. To cultures that conceive of their universe as consisting of tiered cosmic regions, the *axis mundi* is the point of intersection where communication with the spirit world is possible. Certain geographical features, such as caves and sinkholes, are associated with this center and are believed to be imbued with sacred power (Bassie-Sweet 1991; Heyden 1981; Schele and Friedel 1990). The use of vertical shaft caves as mortuary sites in the lower Pecos was a means of returning the dead to the place of origin and the place where the ancestors now reside.

The opening at the top of the crenelated arch in the otherworld journey motif represents the portal to the otherworld. In the natural landscape, the mouth of the sinkhole served as the portal to the supernatural realm—the land of the ancestors. The opening in the crenelated arch, which often has lines emanating outward from the center, also represents the bright light at the end of the tunnel experienced by shamans in their altered state. The light at the end of the tunnel would have been re-created when standing in the bottom of the sinkhole or within a vertical shaft cave, as light poured into the chamber through the earth's surface. The crenelated lines on each side of the portal represent the serpent—the gateway to the otherworld. A passage through openings in the earth's surface, such as sinkholes or vertical shaft caves, symbolizes entrance to the otherworld through the mouth of the serpent, or making the dangerous journey past the two-headed serpent—gatekeeper to the world below, the land of the dead.

Polysemy and Visionary Art

It would be easy to fall into the trap of explaining all crenelated lines as gateway serpents, all anthropomorphs as shamans. These elements, however, are explained as such only in the painted context of other elements in the otherworld journey motif. Crenelated lines are not always gateway serpents, nor are all anthropomorphs shamans. The potential semiotic associations for such visionary images are countless. They are polysemic—that is, they have a diversity of meanings (V. Turner 1967). In *The Dream Seekers,* Lee Irwin (1994) examined 150 years of Plains Indian visionary experiences documented in published and unpublished sources. He stated: "The communication of vision experience is part of a shared context in which the image is primary for the expression of meaning. . . . There is a powerful visual economy at work in which a minimal symbol such as a circle or star can express a maximum of meaning" (Irwin 1994:232).

The wide variety of contexts within which anthropomorphic forms and crenelated lines appear—both in relation to other pictographic elements in a panel and the location of a rock art panel on the landscape—suggests an equally wide variety of possible explanations. Crenelated lines may represent water, mountains, snakes, or any number of worldly or otherworldly manifestations. Anthropomorphs may portray a wide range of supernatural or natural beings—deities, ancestor spirits, mythical beings, shaman, witches, historical figures, and so on. To refer to all anthropomorphic figures as "shamans" or all crenelated lines as "gateway serpents" is to deny the richness, diversity, and complexity of hunter-gatherer belief systems, thereby feeding the stereotype of the "simple primitive."

We should not only honor the polysemic nature of each element present in the journey motif but also recognize that there may be a multiplicity of meanings associated with the motif itself. Visionary imagery is variable and not dogmatically defined; therefore, the image and its symbolic content are always open to new interpretation. The multiple meanings communicated through the visionary image are not always recorded or even explicit in the mind of the seer (Irwin 1994). Therefore, embodied in the otherworld journey motif is an amalgam of ascribed and implied meanings,

as well as a multitude of meanings that were not verbally explicit in the minds of the lower Pecos peoples.

The Work of Art and Artist

Although I have explained the journey motif as a graphic representation of shamanic journeys into the otherworld, the work of the art and of the artist extend beyond graphic representation. The motif does not simply represent shamans' experiences in the otherworld nor is it merely a *reflection* of the myths, histories, economic and political structures, or religious identities of the society within which it was produced. Rather, the art and the artists performed an active role in the creation, continuation, and transformation of every aspect of the lower Pecos sociocultural system—economic, political, social, and ideological.

ROCK ART AND INDIRECT INSTRUCTION

Ju/'hoansi hunter-gatherer artists and their art serve a vital role in the maintenance and transformation of San society in southern Africa (Biesele 1983). Biesele (1983:59) stated that the painter's work should be viewed as "both symbolic in nature and practical in effect." The work performed by expressive forms, such as rock art, may not have been able to be accomplished in any other way; it served to indirectly communicate information necessary for the reproduction of society (Biesele 1983).

Direct instruction and order-giving among hunter-gatherers is rare and is often met with adverse reactions. The reason for this adverse reaction has been attributed to the intensely egalitarian structure of hunter-gatherer societies, a structure that entails extensive food-sharing. All foods obtained are shared equally regardless of whether the recipients spent the day hunting, gathering, or sleeping. "It is not far-fetched to suggest that this force [food-sharing] may have been strong enough for long enough to set constraints on the way that information was best transmitted from person to person and acquired by individuals" (Blurton Jones and Konner 1976:345).

Biesele (1983) suggested that rock paintings, like stories related by storytellers, are developed and utilized as a means of indirect instruction and information exchange within egalitarian societies with oral traditions. These oral traditions, as nonwritten expressive forms of communication, serve to transform individual experiences into shared experiences and individual knowledge into shared knowledge. The sharing of both tangible and intangible resources is essential in egalitarian societies; expressive forms, such as rock art, are vehicles through which the intangible assets (general knowledge about animal behavior, plant habitat, trance experience, etc.) are distributed from the individual to the group without threatening autonomy.

ROCK ART AND
SOCIAL RELATIONS

If the rock art was a means of indirect instruction and information exchange, and I believe it was, what information and instruction were being communicated through the motif, and why was the transmission of this information necessary?

The otherworld journey motif provides information about cosmology and the visionary experiences associated with altered states in a concrete, representational form. This graphic representation is important on several levels. First, it transforms individual experience into shared experience. Biesele (1983:56) noted that among the Ju/'hoansi, "the rendering of individual kergymatic accounts (personal religious revelation) into culturally shared images is a very important process in the religious unity of hunter-

gatherers." The graphic representation of one's journey to the spirit realm is a vehicle through which that experience can be culturally shared. One of the most effective ways of communicating the visionary experience is through visual arts. The otherworld journey motif creates a visible context within which the structure of the cosmos and its supernatural inhabitants can be seen as tangibly present.

The rock art panels of the lower Pecos were part of the living landscape that provided food, shelter, and a connection with the spirit world. The work performed by the otherworld journey motif, therefore, extends beyond simple graphic representation of cosmology and the shamanic experience. The motif also instructs and informs initiate shamans about the trance experience. Prior to a youth's first vision quest, the shaman relates his or her own dream or vision, thus establishing a precedent for visionary experience of the neophyte. Sharing the experience provides neophytes with a context for their upcoming vision experience and the proper context for its future narration (Irwin 1994). Elements of the journey motif are representative of actual neurological processes associated with altered states. As such, the motif contains not just "mythical" information regarding the structure of the cosmos but also factual data regarding the trance experience. The pictorial representation of sensory experiences associated with altered states may have served to reduce anxiety for neophytes and predispose them to a particular visionary experience.

An individual's personal religious revelations are to a large degree culturally informed and mediated: "Initiates have certain experiences in trance because they expect to do so, basing their expectations on other accounts they have heard" (Biesele 1983) and, in the case of rock art, seen. The journey motif, conditions, facilitates, and validates the trance experience. "The image is an opening into the sacred realm of the numinous—dangerous, powerful, and cathartic. . . . The image is metamorphic and transformative. Through its use and manipulation, the shaman could enter into the visionary realm and return with remarkable knowledge" (Irwin 1994:215). The sharing of dream and vision experiences is regarded as a serious religious matter among Native Americans. These experiences are believed to be a form of knowledge and a source of personal empowerment. The mishandling of visionary power for purposes other than originally intended is believed to have potentially devastating repercussions. Lying or exaggerating about the vision experience could result in the visionary's being punished by dream spirits (Irwin 1994).

Individuals who have a history of successful vision experiences, who have been able to successfully communicate the experience, the knowledge gained through the vision, and its associated power to the group in socially recognized forms become religious leaders. Visionary experiences encoded in art have powerful religious associations that, when used correctly, are capable of transforming the very structures of perception, and of informing, validating, and transforming social and religious identity (Driver 1969; Irwin 1994).

Through vision imagery presented in the form of rock art, shamans could negotiate their position within the community, introduce new cultural practices and technologies, and enhance, challenge, or reinforce existing social and religious identities. Rock art, therefore, should not be thought of as a passive prop—decorative or aesthetic in intent—but rather as instrumental, an active agent in the creation, continuation, and transformation of every aspect of the lower Pecos sociocultural system.

Five

NATURE'S BRIDGE TO THE OTHERWORLD

**Perhaps the discovery that certain substances found in nature help man
to move beyond his everyday experiences to "Otherworlds" and the institutionalizing
of these personal ecstatic experiences into an ideological and ritual framework accepted
by the groups as a whole . . . goes back to the beginnings of human culture.**

P. T. FURST, *Flesh of the Gods*

Motifs B and C in Pecos River–style rock art are also associated with otherworld journeys. More specifically, these motifs reflect the use of psychotropic plants by shamans as a sacrament, medicine, and bridge to the supernatural realm.

Antlered Anthropomorphs, Impaled Deer, and Dots: A Pictographic Motif

Pictographic elements of Motif B are composed of antlered anthropomorphs with black dots on the ends of their antler tines, impaled deer, and impaled dots. This recurring motif in lower Pecos art appears at four of the five sites in the study, the exception being Rattlesnake Canyon (41VV180).

The panel at the White Shaman site (41VV124) contains the clearest example of Motif B (fig. 5.1). I spent approximately seventy hours in the field sketching and photographing pictographs at this site. In the course of producing a scale color rendering of the White Shaman panel, I recognized that this recurring motif occurs in the context of a larger composition. In fact, the vast majority of the images in the White Shaman panel are part of a well-organized composition—not simply a random placement of pictographic elements. As a composition, the White Shaman panel offers a unique opportunity to consider the recurring motif within the context of other imagery in the panel—as part of a greater whole (plate 2).

The rock art panel contains five black and red, noncentrastyled, anthropomorphic figures that are placed close to equidistance from one another along the four-by-eight-meter panel. Each figure is approximately one meter in height and is holding a slender, black, torchlike object with red tip. Skeletonized anthropomorphs, zoomorphs, and other

FIG. 5.1 White Shaman (41VV124). Impaled deer, impaled dots, and an antlered anthropomorph with dots on its antler tines. The anthropomorph is passing through a crenelated arch, which I interpret in chapter 4 as a portal to the otherworld. Scale 1 cm ≈ 23 cm.

enigmatic figures surround each of the black and red anthropomorphs. More than one hundred circles or dots cover the shelter wall and decorate the figures. Motif B is located at the left end of the panel where, just beneath an impaled deer that is covered with black dots, there is an antlered anthropomorph whose tines are tipped with black dots. The antlered anthropomorph is superimposed over the upper part of a large undulating arch. This anthropomorph is the only one depicted with a weapon—in this case, an atlatl. Close to the antlered anthropomorph and the impaled deer are red dots impaled by spears or dart shafts.

Just above the impaled dots is an object resembling a whisk that consists of a straight line with numerous branching lines projecting from one end. A white line extends the entire length of the panel, uniting the five anthropomorphic figures and other pictographic elements. At the far left end of the panel, this line changes to black.

At Panther Cave (41VV83) and Mystic Shelter (41VV612) two elements in Motif B are present. It is possible that all three elements were once included in the panels. If so, they are no longer visible because of overpainting or damage to the pictographs. At least seven-

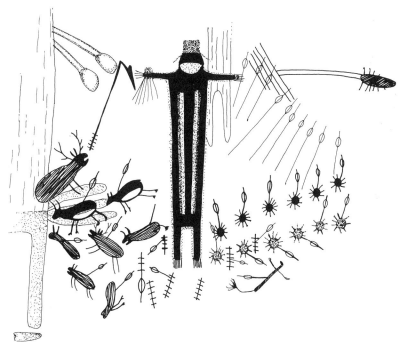

FIG. 5.2   (Top) Panther Cave (41vv83). Impaled dots and impaled deer. Scale 1cm ≈ 25cm.

FIG. 5.3   (Bottom) Cedar Springs (41vv696). Antlered anthropomorph with dots on the tips of its antlers. The anthropomorph is located just beneath a crenelated arch. Scale 1cm ≈ 8cm.

teen deer are represented at Panther Cave and most are impaled. Found in close proximity to the impaled deer, and in some cases intermingled with them, are impaled dots. At least fifteen impaled red and yellow dots are illustrated, each with lines radiating outward (fig. 5.2). No antlered anthropomorphs have been identified in the panel. At least five impaled deer and two antlered anthropomorphs are depicted at Mystic Shelter. The body of one antlered anthropomorph is covered with black dots, and its antler tines are tipped in black. The other antlered figure is so badly damaged by water seepage that details of the figure are difficult to determine. No impaled dots have been identified in the panel.

At Cedar Springs (41vv696), antlers of the skeletonized anthropomorph are decorated with black dots on the end of each antler tine

(fig. 5.3). Depictions of at least twenty-one deer, more than half of which have been impaled, are also included in the Cedar Springs and Cedar Springs annex panels. At least nineteen antler racks bedecked with black dots have been identified within the main Cedar Springs panel, and at least eight impaled

FIG. 5.4   Cedar Springs (41vv696). Deer with dots decorating its antler tines. Scale 1cm ≈ 1.3cm.

black dots have been identified in the Cedar Springs annex panel (see fig. 3.10). Antlers of a thirteen-centimeter deer in the annex, perhaps Red Linear style, are decorated with dots on the ends of each antler tine (fig. 5.4).

Shamans, Sacred Deer, and Peyote: An Ethnographic Motif

While conducting a review of the ethnographic literature on cultures within northern Mexico and the American Southwest, I recognized a motif similar to that identified within the lower Pecos pictographs. In the literature, the corresponding motif is associated with peyotism—the ritual use of *Lophophora williamsii* (peyote cactus). The elements of the ethnographic motif include: (1) the use of peyote by shamans as sacrament, medicine, and bridge to the otherworld; (2) the uniting of peyote and deer into an inseparable sacred symbol; and (3) the sacrifice of peyote/deer in rain-bringing ceremonies. Further study resulted in the identification of additional sim-

ilarities between the pictographs contained in the White Shaman panel and an annual Huichol pilgrimage to collect the sacred peyote cactus (Boyd 1998; Boyd and Dering 1996).

BOTANY OF PEYOTE

Peyote is a spherical, spineless, chalky blue green cactus with a height of less than five centimeters and a diameter of seldom more than six to eight centimeters (fig. 5.5). It is most frequently found in shallow, rocky upland soils under the thorny shrub canopy provided by other plants such as mesquite and acacia. Peyote grows in clusters from a tuberous taproot that is associated with a much larger nurse plant. During drought conditions, peyote crowns shrink, descending below ground to reduce exposure to transpiration losses. When the rains return, the cactus swells and rises slightly above the surface of the soil (Benitez 1975; Boke and Anderson 1970; Bruhn and Holmstedt 1974; Morgan 1983).

    The plant's geographic range is primarily in northeastern and central Mexico and along the

FIG. 5.5   Peyote *(Lophophora williamsii);* about 3 centimeters in
diameter. Photograph by J. Phil Dering.

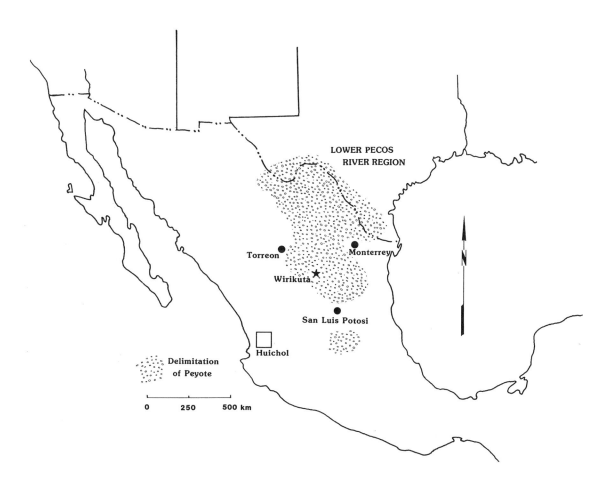

FIG. 5.6   Delimitation of peyote in North America. Modified from Morgan (1983).

Texas borderlands (fig. 5.6) (Boke and Anderson 1970; Morgan 1983). In the lower Pecos River region, modern peyote populations are located on south-facing slopes overlooking the western side of the Pecos River Canyon, on the uplands above Seminole Canyon just east of the Pecos River, as well as in the area of Langtry, Texas. Many more populations are probably within a few miles of the rockshelters in this study, but locating them is difficult because of restricted access to private land.

The cactus is harvested by slicing off the small exposed crown. When dried, segments of the cactus resemble hard, brownish disks referred to as peyote buttons (fig. 5.7). Of the more than thirty alkaloids chemically identified in peyote, the major active alkaloid—mescaline—is capable of producing psychic effects and hallucinations in humans (Aberle 1966; E. Anderson 1996; Bruhn and Holm-

stedt 1974; Litovitz 1983). Taken in small quantities, less than 5 mg/kg, peyote produces wakefulness and mild analgesia. It also suppresses the sexual drive, reduces appetite, and allays thirst (Aberle 1966; Klüver 1966; La Barre 1975; Schultes 1938). Each button contains on average 45 mg of mescaline; thus, four to twelve buttons must be consumed to produce vivid visual hallucinations, including reports of shimmering intensification of color and texture, frequent geometric imagery, and distortions in body image and depth perception. Although peyote intoxication is most commonly associated with visual hallucinations, auditory and tactile hallucinations, as well as a variety of synesthesia, have also been reported (E. Anderson 1996; Bye 1979; Klüver 1966; Litovitz 1983; Schultes 1969; Siegel 1984).

To many Native Americans, peyote is not a

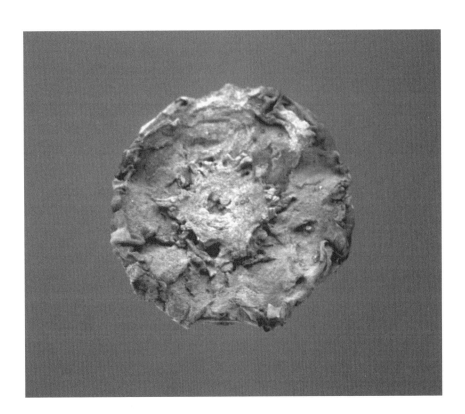

FIG. 5.7   Peyote button recovered from a rockshelter near Mile Canyon in the lower
Pecos River region; about 7 centimeters in diameter. (In private collection.)
Photograph by J. Phil Dering.

hallucinogenic drug but a religious sacrament. Through the centuries, peyote has been used by Native Americans more for its therapeutic properties than for its vision-producing properties. According to Edward Anderson, "The primary use of sacred plants by most indigenous people in North America has always been religious and at the same time medicinal because religion and medicine have not been separated" (E. Anderson 1996:107). In Mexico, peyote is used to protect individuals from sickness—it forms a barrier against all that is evil. In the United States, the primary use of peyote is to treat individuals after they become ill. Peyote is reported to cure nearly everything, including tuberculosis, pneumonia, rheumatism, scarlet fever, venereal disease, diabetes, influenza, snake bites, cancer, insanity, broken bones, and many more ailments (Aberle 1966; E. Anderson 1996; Bye 1979; Hultkrantz 1997; La Barre 1975). Scientists have responded to the widespread claims of peyote's therapeutic value by searching for substances in peyote that may be medically significant. One of their most interesting discoveries is that of a crystalline substance, "peyocactin," which is believed to have antibiotic qualities. Peyocactin has been demonstrated to have a definite in vitro antiseptic action against a wide variety of microorganisms.

ORIGINS OF PEYOTISM

Pre-Columbian groups in southern Texas and throughout northern Mexico are known to have utilized peyote in religious ceremonies (Hultkrantz 1997; La Barre 1975; Stewart 1987). In the nineteenth century peyote use spread northward to Oklahoma where the modern peyote religion of the Native American Church became formalized during the 1880s (Hultkrantz 1997; Stewart 1987). Considerable controversy exists regarding the origins of peyotism and the content of the earlier cult from which it emerged (Campbell 1958;

Howard 1957, 1960; Hultkrantz 1997; Opler 1937, 1938, 1945; Slotkin 1951, 1955; Stewart 1987; Troike 1962). From preconquest times to early in the nineteenth century, various groups located in Mexico and Texas either utilized or were familiar with the peyote cactus. These groups include the Aztec, Zacateco, Tarascan, Cazcan, Guachichil, Huichol, Lagunero, Tepehuan, Tepecano, Cora, Acaxee, Tamaulipeco, Coahuilteco, Tarahumara, Opata, Akmiel O'odham (Pima), Tohono O'odham (Papago), Yaqui, Jumano, Julimeno, Lipan Apache, Carrizo, Tonkawa, Karankawa, Mescalero Apache, Caddo, Otomi, and Tlascalan (Hrdlicka 1908; Shonle 1925; Stewart 1987).

Although peyote use among tribes in Mexico was most prominent among the Huichol, it was also well known among the Opata and the Yaqui. The Tepecano used peyote obtained from the Huichol for medicinal and ceremonial purposes. The Tohono O'odham (Papago) and Akmiel O'odham (Pima) also used peyote for medicinal and, most probably, ceremonial purposes as well (Hrdlicka 1908).

Peyotism in the United States is recognized as having its origins in northern Mexico and southern Texas along the Rio Grande (Hultkrantz 1997; La Barre 1975; Stewart 1974, 1987), near the northern limits of the natural growth range of peyote. During historic times, various Indian groups such as Comanches and Kiowas and tribes from Oklahoma journeyed to the lower Pecos region to harvest peyote for ceremonial use. The Comanches and the Kiowas reportedly collected peyote along the Rio Grande and Pecos River (Slotkin 1951, 1955; Stewart 1987). According to Jack R. Skiles, a botanist living in the area of Langtry, Texas, "Indians from Oklahoma made trips to Langtry for many years (during the 1930s) gathering peyote for use in their religious ceremonies" (Skiles, cited in Stewart 1987:13).

The earliest historical reference to peyotism

was made in the 1560s by Fray Bernardino de Sahagún. In his *General History of the Things of New Spain,* he credits the primitive nomadic tribes of northern Mexico, the "Teochichimeca," with discovering the hallucinogenic properties of the peyote cactus. The Teochichimeca peyote ceremony described by Sahagún shares many features with peyote ceremonies conducted by modern Huichol Indians of northern Mexico (Furst 1972; La Barre 1975; Myerhoff 1974; Stewart 1987). Schaefer and Furst (1996:23) maintained that the contemporary Huichol peyote ritual is "the last intact survivor of a very old Chichimec/Desert Culture peyote complex." Ancestors of the modern Huichol are believed to have migrated as nomadic Chichimec hunters into the Sierra Madre Occidentals from a northern homeland (Furst 1972; Schaefer and Furst 1996).

HUICHOL PEYOTISM

The peyote hunt is at the core of the Huichol belief system. It unites peyote, deer, and maize into one inseparable, sacred symbol. Deer, peyote, and maize are so intimately interwoven that the Huichol believe that maize is deer, peyote is deer, and maize is peyote; one cannot exist without the others (Furst 1972, 1976, 1978; La Barre 1975; Lumholtz 1900; Myerhoff 1974; Schaefer and Furst 1996).

Huichol religion is complex; however, the driving force in ritual practices is the desire for rain. In Huichol myths, both peyote and rain spring from the forehead of the deer. Without deer, there would be no peyote and no rain; consequently, there would be no maize. Peyote is therefore sacrificed each year to Grandfather Fire to ensure rain and a bountiful crop (Lumholtz 1900, 1902). The only peyote that may be used as a sacrifice in these ceremonies is peyote the Huichol have obtained from their sacred homeland, Wirikúta. In myth and possibly in history, Wirikúta

is the place from which the Ancient Ones came before settling in the Sierra Madre Occidentals in north-central Mexico. Each year preceding the spring rain-bringing ceremonies, small bands of Huichol unite and set out upon a 480-kilometer pilgrimage across the desert, journeying northeast to the land of their origin where the peyote grows (see fig. 5.6) (Benitez 1975; Furst 1972; Furst and Myerhoff 1966; Lumholtz 1902).

In order to enter the sacred homeland, each pilgrim must be transformed into a spirit being. It is the responsibility of the shaman, or *mara'akame,* to assist in this transformation and to assign a new name to each pilgrim. The shaman who leads the group on the hunt always becomes Grandfather Fire. He carries the antlers of the Huichol divine ancestor Kauyumári, or Sacred Deer Person. Kauyumári, the intermediary between the shaman and the gods, serves as the guide and protector of the pilgrims along the journey (Benitez 1975; Furst 1972; Lumholtz 1900; Myerhoff 1974). The Huichol describe him as follows: "We call him *Kauyumári.* We call him *Maxa Kwaxí.* It is all one. *Kauyumári* aids Grand-father Fire. He aids Father Sun. He guides the *mara'akame* in what must be done. So that the peyote can be hunted. So that the *mara'akame* can take the peyote from the horns of the deer, there in *Wirikúta*" (Myerhoff 1974:87). Kauyumári is envisaged either in the form of a deer or as a person wearing antlers. The Huichol believe that when the deer-god descended from heaven, he brought peyote on his antlers to the sacred homeland, leaving the divine peyote cactus behind in his tracks (see fig. 5.8). It is also believed that Kauyumári uses his antlers to open the portal to the otherworld on the peyote pilgrimage (Benitez 1975; Furst 1972; Myerhoff 1974).

Before the pilgrims can be completely transformed into divine beings they must experience purification and confession. The primary function of this ritual is "to transform

FIG. 5.8 Huichol yarn painting by Chavelo González de la Cruz, illustrating the birth of peyote from the antlers and body of the Great Deer in Wirikúta. Partial rendering of yarn painting redrawn from Lemaistre (1996).

the participants spiritually by making them new" (Myerhoff 1974:132). Sexual misdeeds are the only actions confessed during the ceremony. Each participant publicly declares his or her sexual transgressions. The shaman makes a knot in a husk fiber cord for each transgression mentioned. After all pilgrims have confessed, the shaman throws the knotted cord in the fire. By this action, transgressions have been absolved and the pilgrims are no longer considered mortal. To signify a new beginning and unity among the pilgrims, the shaman removes from his pouch a fresh cactus fiber cord that each pilgrim is instructed to grasp. The shaman scorches the cord over the fire before placing it back in his pouch (Benitez 1975; Myerhoff 1974). When they arrive in the land of Wirikúta, the sacred cord is knotted by each pilgrim; it is unknotted at the end of their journey home (Furst 1972; Lumholtz 1900; Myerhoff 1974).

Once the confessions and transformations are complete, the group leaves the village in

single file. The shaman-leader goes first, carrying the bow and arrows with which the first peyote will be shot. He also carries deer antlers, which represent Kauyumári (Lumholtz 1900; Myerhoff 1974). Strict attention is given to preserving the order of the pilgrims as they proceed in single file. This order must be maintained no matter how awkward or inconvenient, just as their ancestors did on the First Peyote Hunt (Benitez 1975; Furst 1974; Lumholtz 1900, 1902; Myerhoff 1974). Candles are an important element in the peyote pilgrimage. At designated points along the journey to Wirikúta, the pilgrims display offerings they have brought to the peyote. They stand before their offerings while holding candles toward the ascending sun (Benitez 1975; Furst 1972; Myerhoff 1974).

About midmorning, after arriving in the sacred homeland of Wirikúta, the shaman signals for the hunt to begin. The pilgrims fan out across the desert, breaking their single file order as they search for the peyote/deer.

Myerhoff (1974:153) describes the pilgrims' behavior as "precisely that of stalking an animal." Once the shaman has found the peyote/deer, he takes aim and shoots it with an arrow. Bursts of color like a rainbow are said to spurt upward from the slain peyote/deer. The colored rays, called the *kupuri,* represent the soul of the peyote and of the deer. The shaman coaxes the soul back into the peyote/deer with his sacred feather plumes (Benitez 1975; Furst 1972; Myerhoff 1974). The pilgrims then proceed to gather peyote to take home. After a sufficient amount has been collected, the peyote is sorted, cleaned, and packed. The shaman selects five of the finest peyotes, each with five sections. The number five, which signifies the four cardinal points and the center, is sacred among the Huichol. It also stands for completion. The five peyotes are strung together and hung upon the antlers of Kauyumári. The next day, the pilgrims begin their long journey home (Benitez 1975; Furst 1972; Myerhoff 1974).

Pictographic Evidence of Peyotism

My review of the literature demonstrated similarities between Motif B, and myth and religious practices surrounding the ritual use of peyote by the Huichol Indians of northern Mexico. It also revealed striking similarities between remaining elements in the White Shaman composition and the Huichol peyote pilgrimage and hunt. Based upon the semblances identified, I offer the following hypothesis for motif B: when found in association, antlered anthropomorphs with black dots on the ends of their antler tines, impaled deer, and impaled dots signify a metaphorical relationship between deer and peyote. The recurrence of this motif suggests that it was a prominent component in lower Pecos rituals involving peyote during the Archaic period.

WHITE SHAMAN REVISITED

Specific elements of the Pecos River–style rock art are similar to elements in the Huichol ritual peyote pilgrimage. Virtually every major aspect of the ritual has a corresponding rock art representation, and virtually every pictographic element at White Shaman can be linked to some aspect of the ritual.

1. Five black and red anthropomorphic figures extend the length of the panel, each approximately the same size and equidistance apart. The artist(s) of the White Shaman rock art panel utilized the full expanse of canvas provided on the shelter wall. The black and red anthropomorphs are placed evenly across the panel, analogous to the strict single file order maintained by the Huichol during their peyote pilgrimage.

2. Long, slender, black objects with red tips are associated with each of the five anthropomorphs. These red-tipped objects are analogous to candles held up by the pilgrims toward the ascending sun while they are making offerings to the peyote at various points along their journey. In the rock art panel, these objects represent torches rather than candles.

3. Skeletonized anthropomorphs, zoomorphs, and other enigmatic figures are associated with each of the five black and red anthropomorphs, which appear to be going through a metamorphosis. This is analogous to the transformation of the pilgrims into spirit-beings before beginning their journey to the sacred homeland to hunt peyote. Guiding the pilgrims in this transformation are the skeletonized depictions of the shaman and his spirit helpers. Modern Huichol artists depict shamans and spirit beings in a skeletonized fashion in yarn paintings (Furst 1978:23). Since the five black and red anthropomorphs are *not* depicted in a skele-

tonized fashion, they represent the pilgrims before their transformation into spirit beings.

4. A white line extends the entire length of the panel and unites the five anthropomorphic figures. At the left end of the panel, the line changes to black. This white line uniting the anthropomorphs is analogous to the cactus-fiber cord used by the Huichol shaman to unify all pilgrims following purification and confession. At one end of the white line, the color changes to black, possibly to symbolize the scorching of the cord by the Huichol shaman. The number of anthropomorphs is also significant. Among the Huichol, five is a sacred number that represents completion. The pilgrims, following their transformation and confession, are considered perfected and complete.

5. An antlered anthropomorph is superimposed over the top of a large undulating arch; it is the only anthropomorph in the panel associated with a weapon—in this case, an atlatl. At the far left end of the panel, passing through the motif representing the otherworld, is a skeletonized, antlered anthropomorph. The antler tines of the headdress are decorated with small

black dots, analogous to the peyote buttons brought to the people on the tines of the Huichol divine ancestor, Kauyumári. This figure, the only anthropomorph in the panel associated with a weapon, is analogous to the shaman-leader who carries both the antlers of Kauyumári to open the otherworld portal and the weapon to shoot the first peyote/deer. This may also be an indication that the panel is to be read from left to right.

6. Impaled dots, impaled deer decorated with dots, and elements resembling whisks or feather plumes are also represented at this site. There are more than one hundred dots in the White Shaman panel. Black dots are depicted on the bodies of the anthropomorphs and are also free-floating throughout the panel. There are at least six impaled red dots. The clearest of these appear on the left end of the panel above the antlered anthropomorph. These impaled dots are analogous to the peyote/deer shot by the Huichol shaman. The impaled deer covered with large black dots closely resembles depictions of the peyote/deer in Huichol sacred art (figs. 5.8 and 5.9). The Huichol decorate the body of the deer with either dots or flowers to represent the peyote

FIG. 5.9   Huichol god disk. Redrawn from Lumholtz (1900).

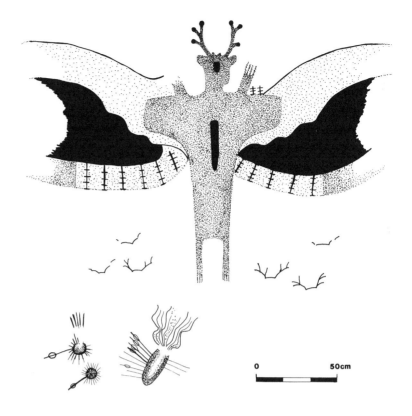

FIG. 5.10 Fate Bell (41vv74). Winged, antlered anthropomorph associated with impaled dots and antler racks.

0   50cm

button The deer, according to Myerhoff (1974:199), "is the most sacred and magical animal of the Huichol. He gave them peyote in the First Hunt and reappears during subsequent hunts, bringing peyote, which is conceptualized as either remaining behind in his footsteps or as growing from his horns and tail." Found in close proximity to the impaled dots and impaled deer is an element resembling the feather plume used by the shaman to coax the soul back into the peyote/deer after it has been shot with the arrow.

RECURRING PATTERNS IN PICTOGRAPHS AND ETHNOGRAPHIES

The association of peyote with deer in the ethnographic literature is not restricted to Huichol peyotism, nor is the motif association of impaled deer, impaled dots, and antlered anthropomorphs with black dots on the ends

of antler tines restricted to sites included in this study. These pictographic elements have been identified in association with one another at other sites as well. At Fate Bell Shelter (41vv74) in Seminole Canyon, the antler tines of a winged antlered anthropomorph are tipped with black dots (fig. 5.10). The winged, antlered anthropomorph itself may be understood through analogy. According to the Huichol, deer have the ability to fly (Myerhoff 1974:201). The sacred deer that brought the First Peyote to the ancestors flew from the heavens with peyote on his antler tines. Found in close proximity to the winged, antlered anthropomorph are impaled dots bursting with color and numerous depictions of antler racks. The colorful impaled dots are analogous to the Huichol description of the soul of the deer escaping as colored rays from the peyote after it is shot by the shaman.

The association of black dots on antler tines with impaled deer and dots is also seen on a panel located near Black Cave (41vv76) in

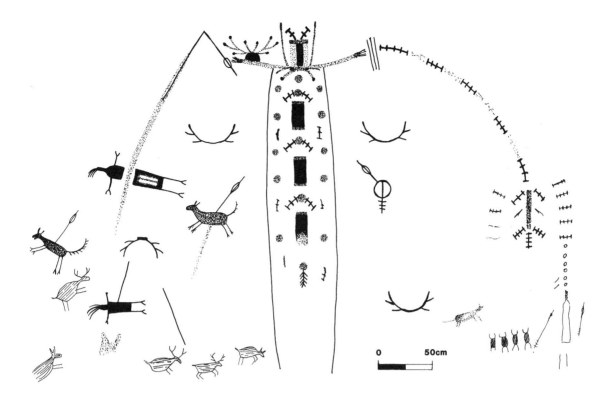

FIG. 5.11 Black Cave (41vv76). Black dots on the ends of antler tines, impaled deer, and an impaled dot are found in association.

Pressa Canyon, a tributary of Seminole Canyon (fig. 5.11). The Black Cave panel supports further analogies with Huichol conceptions of the peyote/deer and rain-bringing. Located approximately three meters to the right of the antlered anthropomorph is another anthropomorph surrounded by impaled deer (fig. 5.12). Above the anthropomorph is an antler rack with rainbow-like rays extending from it. This may be analogous to the Huichol notion of rain springing from the forehead of the deer, or of the colored rays representing the soul of the peyote/deer trying to escape after being shot.

Interestingly, the motif has also been identified in the Red Linear– and Red Monochrome–style art that emerged two thousand years after the Pecos River style. Dots have been clearly identified on the antler tines of what could be classified as a Red Linear deer in Cedar Springs annex (41vv696) (see fig. 5.4) and perhaps also in a Red Linear panel located

in Pressa Canyon (41vv201) (fig. 5.13). The dots on the tines of the Red Linear deer in Pressa Canyon may have resulted from spalling of surrounding paint. Located to the left of the deer, however, is an anthropomorph holding what resembles a gourd rattle in his left hand and two impaled dots with his right hand. Gourd rattles are a major component of Native American Church peyote rituals (Stewart 1987). The two impaled dots in this Red Linear panel may be analogous to the slain peyote/deer. At Painted Canyon (41vv78), a large Red Monochrome deer is painted with a design very similar to the Huichol depiction of the peyote/deer (fig. 5.14). Although these three sites are isolated examples of this motif from more recent pictographs in the region, further research may reveal additional sites with the same motif. Since we have contemporary, ethnographic accounts of a peyote/deer relationship (Schaefer and Furst 1996; Underhill 1952), the presence of this motif in more recent pictographs is not surprising.

Other groups besides the Huichol associate peyote with deer. The antiquity of this association is suggested in Zapotec material culture. An effigy snuffing pipe, about 2,500 years old, from Monte Albán, Mexico, depicts a reclining deer holding a peyote cactus in its mouth (Furst 1976). The association of deer with peyote, although less direct, is also present among the Papago. Ruth Underhill (1969:264) observed that Papago "shamans owned love magic. A 'mushroom' which corresponds with the Huichol description of peyote, was a strong love charm. A man stalked it like a deer, and shot it with an arrow before it had a chance to disappear into the ground." Also according to Underhill (1969), there is a mys-

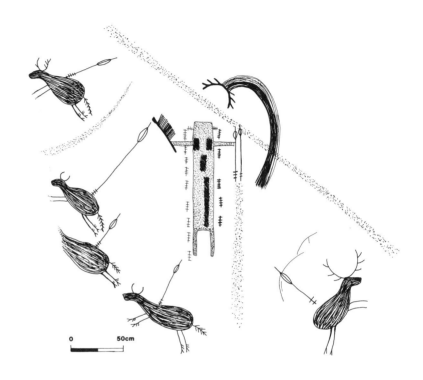

FIG. 5.12   Black Cave (41vv76). Impaled deer located approximately 3 meters to the right of the panel illustrated in FIG. 5.9.

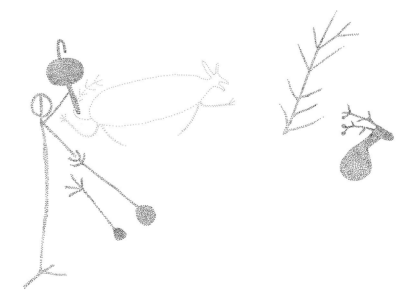

FIG. 5.13   Pressa Canyon Red Linear site (41vv201). Red Linear anthropomorph holding object resembling impaled dot found in association with deer. Scale 1cm ≈ 3cm.

terious connection between an unidentified plant used by the Papago as an intoxicant, known as *pihuri,* and deer. She suggests that the Papago *pihuri* may be analogous to the Huichol *hikuri* (peyote).

The association of deer and peyote is also present in ritual foot races conducted by various Mexican groups. Use of peyote to increase stamina during ritual racing is known among the Tarahumara, Huichol, Tamaulipecan, and Axacee tribes. The Tarahumara and Huichol carry the peyote/deer during ritual foot races. The association of deer and peyote is even more direct among the Axacee, who tie strips of deer hide or hooves to their insteps during a race to help them climb hills (La Barre 1975; Lumholtz 1902). The peyote/deer relationship is also represented in the modern peyote religion of the Native American Church. In the United States many members of the Native American Church make a pilgrimage to southern Texas or northern Mexico to collect pey-

ote plants for use in ceremonies. The peyote will not reveal itself to the pilgrims until after they have prayed. At that time, "it may appear in the form of a man or deer, leaving the plants behind" (Underhill 1952:144).

Deer, Peyote, Maize, and Rain: A Natural Fit

Today, as in 1900 when Carl Lumholtz conducted research in Mesoamerica, the Huichol sacrifice the peyote/deer as an offering to the gods to bring rain and insure against drought. They believe peyote must be offered to the gods every year "or they would be unable to catch deer: consequently it would not rain and they would have no corn" (Lumholtz 1900:23). Why would hunter-gatherers living along waterways of the lower Pecos region sacrifice the peyote/deer in rain-bringing

FIG. 5.14   Painted Canyon Red Monochrome site (41vv78). Depiction of deer and canine-like animal. Scale 1cm ≈ 13cm.

ceremonies? And why are these seemingly disparate elements combined in pictographs and ethnographic literature? A look at the effects of peyote intoxication and the ecology of deer and peyote reveals that these seemingly disparate elements are not so disparate after all.

NEUROPHYSIOLOGY AND THE PEYOTE/DEER RELATIONSHIP

Peyote is widely used as a stimulant in Mexico. Individuals who take peyote claim that it allows them to overcome great fatigue and endure hunger and thirst for several days (Aberle 1966; La Barre 1975; Schultes 1938). These physiological effects of peyote intoxication represent the physical basis for the connection of peyote with deer and rain. I suggest that as an appetite suppressor, peyote is meat—more specifically, it is deer meat. As for its ability to alleviate thirst, peyote is water or rain.

During peyote intoxication, individuals maintain consciousness and are able to control their limbs and senses (Schultes 1938). Onlookers have described them as "jumping like a deer" (La Barre 1975:17). Lumholtz, referring to the Huichol, noted that "although an Indian feels drunk after eating a quantity of *hikuli* [peyote], . . . he maintains the balance of his body even better than under normal conditions, and he will walk along the edge of precipices without becoming dizzy" (1903:138). Eating peyote, therefore, not only satisfies hunger like deer meat does but also can cause one to behave like a deer.

AN ECOLOGICAL EXPLANATION

A ritual similar to that of the Huichol may have existed among prehistoric hunter-gatherers of the lower Pecos River region. The ecological relationship between peyote, deer, and rain can be used to explain the peyote/deer/rain complex among hunter-gatherers of the lower Pecos and perhaps explain the relationship of these three elements in ethnographic literature.

Rainfall in the lower Pecos occurs primarily during summer and often takes the form of sporadic, torrential rains of short duration. These rains increase the production of desert ephemerals and trigger leafing and flowering of important forage plants and fruit-bearing shrubs. The peyote/deer would have been sacrificed to bring rain not for crops but for an increase in desert plants and thus the animals that forage on them.

In the Chihuahuan Desert, deer ecologists have demonstrated that deer travel rapidly to a given area soon after rainfall to eat the emerging vegetation (Cooke 1993). Deer have been shown to leave dry-season homes where no rain has fallen and travel as far as thirty-two kilometers to an area that received rain three days earlier. Deer do not migrate in search of more nutritious forage or a better habitat but for the feed that appears after rain. When rain comes, deer also come, sometimes from considerable distances (Rautenstrauch and Krausman 1989). Therefore, rainfall increases not only plant food availability but also game availability.

Rainfall also brings peyote. Peyote has an extensive growing range within the Chihuahuan Desert from central Mexico to southern Texas, including the lower Pecos River region. The peyote cactus grows in shrub microenvironments on east- and south-facing slopes to receive moisture from prevailing gulf winds. During dry periods, peyote descends below the ground surface and is difficult to find. Immediately after a rain, however, the peyote swells and becomes visible on the surface of the ground (Benitez 1975; Morgan 1983). Thus when rain comes, deer come, and peyote appears on the ground where the deer have been feeding on fresh vegetation. As the Huichol say, wherever the deer has stepped, peyote will grow in its tracks. The inclusion of maize in the peyote/deer complex by the marginally agricultural Huichol may represent an extension of the already existing relationship identified by hunter-gatherers between rainfall and the arrival of peyote, deer, and wild plant foods. Another connection has been noted between peyote and deer. R. E. Schultes (1938:699) proposed that "[p]eyote plants are normally unicephalous, but age and injury may cause them to become polycephalous, assuming bizarre shapes, often resembling a deer hoof imprint, a circumstance which may account for the close association of peyote with the deer in Mexican mythology."

My contention is that the lower Pecos shaman/artists used rock paintings to indirectly instruct members of society about ecological relationships, such as the effects of rain on animal and plant behavior—knowledge that was necessary for successful exploitation of the hunting and gathering niche. Further, the shaman may also have been able to indirectly influence social cooperation regarding the control of scarce resources through the art and associated rituals. Conservation ethics are reflected in spiritual beliefs (Kelly 1995). Among the San, "trance was the liminal area within which the [San] medicine men accomplished their articulations of ecological reality (e.g., scattered rainfall) with social necessity (bands cooperating within a band nexus for maximization of resources)" (Biesele 1983:55).

Peyote in Archaeological Deposits

Additional evidence supporting the presence of peyotism in the lower Pecos comes from the archaeological record. George Martin (1933), an archaeologist working in the lower Pecos region during the 1930s, reported having frequently found peyote in the deposits of several rockshelters located on the Pecos River near Shumla, Texas. These rockshelters are collectively referred to as Shumla Caves. Direct AMS assays on peyote excavated from Shumla Cave No. 5 (41VV115) have yielded ages 5175 ± 35 B.P. (CAMS 83631) and 5185 ± 35 B.P. (CAMS 83632). Peyote was also reported by Woolsey at Fields Shelter and by Sayles in several Texas sites (Campbell 1958; Sayles 1935).

Several items of material culture recovered from Shumla Cave excavations are similar to paraphernalia used in peyote ceremonies by various aboriginal groups. These include rasping sticks made from either bone or wood, a rattle made from deer scapula, a pouch and reed tubes containing cedar incense, and feather plumes (La Barre 1975; Lumholtz 1900, 1902; Schultes 1937; Stewart 1987).

Peyote has also been recovered from a rockshelter in Coahuila, Mexico. Nine peyote buttons strung on a cord were excavated from CM-79, a burial cave located about fifty miles west of Cuatro Cienegas. Radiocarbon dates obtained for this site fall within the Late Prehistoric period, 1200–920 B.P. (Taylor 1988).

Mescalism—A Predecessor to Peyotism in the Lower Pecos?

The origins of modern peyotism in the United States remain unclear. Åke Hultkrantz (1997:31) maintained that "Mexican tribal peyote ritualism constituted the transition to the Plains peyote rite," and "the Coahuiltec—living on both sides of the eastern Rio Grande—are most likely to have been the transmitters." Ruecking (1954:337) asserts not only that peyotism was present among the Coahuiltecans as early as the 1500s but also that the "peyote complex was diffused from the Coahuiltecan area to other groups of Mexico" and then "in much later times to the Plains of the United States." Beals (1973) limited the ceremonial use of peyote before 1750 to northern Mexico and suggested that the modern peyote cult stemmed from a ceremonial setting in that area.

La Barre (1975) also suggested that the ceremonial origin of peyotism was northeastern Mexico and argued that mescalism—the ritual use of the mescal bean *(Sophora secundiflora)*—predates peyotism in the United States and Mexico. Some researchers further suggested that mescalism not only predates peyotism but also greatly influenced development of the modern peyote religion (Howard 1957, 1960; Hultkrantz 1997). They maintained that peyote gradually replaced the dangerous mescal bean, until ultimately a distinct ceremonial peyote complex was established. Troike (1962:947) argued, however, that mescalism was not ever really a cult because, as far as we know, the mescal bean was never an object of worship. Stewart (1980) and Merrill (1977) asserted that there is no evidence to suggest that a mescal bean ceremonial complex led to the development of the peyote religion. The pictographs of the lower Pecos River region were entered into this debate by T. N. Campbell (1958). In support of La Barre's argument for mescalism as a predecessor to peyotism, Campbell noted the presence of mescal beans in archaeological deposits of the lower Pecos River region, and identified similarities between the mescal bean medicine society and the Pecos River–style pictographs.

BOTANY OF TEXAS MOUNTAIN LAUREL

The Texas mountain laurel *(Sophora secundiflora)* is an evergreen shrub or small tree of the legume family (Fabaceae) native to northern Mexico and the adjacent southwestern United States. In the lower Pecos region, it is a common shrub in canyons, where the showy, bluish purple flowers mature into a hard, woody legume containing red seeds known as mescal beans (fig. 5.15). The seeds of *Sophora secundiflora* contain narcotic, poisonous, quinolizidine alkaloids, including cystine, that produce a variety of physiological effects. The symptomatology of poisoning through their ingestion includes nausea, vomiting, diarrhea, excitement, muscle paralysis, insensitivity to pain, delirium, convulsions, coma, and occasionally death through respiratory failure. The nature, duration, and intensity of the effects of mescal bean intoxication depend primarily on the number of seeds consumed and the manner in which they are prepared for ingestion (Hatfield et al. 1977; Merrill 1977).

There is no evidence that any mescal bean alkaloids can directly induce hallucinations, however, the mescal bean does serve in creating the context within which visions take place (Hatfield et al. 1977; Merrill 1977). Merrill (1977:4) stated that "the visions seem to have resulted from the combined impact of several factors, including the physiological effects of the mescal bean alkaloids, the dramatic and frequently intense sensory stimulation characteristic of the ceremonial contexts in which mescal beans were consumed, and the vision-seeker's belief and expectation that visions were both possible and likely to occur in such contexts."

MESCAL BEANS IN THE ARCHAEOLOGICAL RECORD

Archaeologists and anthropologists have explored the ritual significance of Texas mountain laurel (Adovasio and Fry 1976; Campbell 1958; Merrill 1977). In the archaeological record, mescal beans have been recovered from cultural deposits of numerous prehistorically inhabited rockshelters in the lower Pecos region, ranging in age from 8000 B.P. to the Historic period. Major rockshelter sites from which seeds or pod fragments have been recovered include Fate Bell Shelter (41VV74), Coontail Spin (41VV82), Zopilote Cave (41VV216), Eagle Cave (41VV167), and Hinds Cave (41VV456) (Campbell 1947; Davenport 1938; Dering 1979; Holden 1937; Martin 1933).

FIG. 5.15   Mescal beans. Seeds of the Texas mountain laurel *(Sophora secundiflora)*.
Photograph by J. Phil Dering.

Despite the widespread occurrence of mescal bean, archaeological evidence provides little insight regarding how the beans were used by prehistoric peoples of the region. Only two sites yielded mescal bean specimens that allude to its utilization. Three longitudinally split mescal beans were attached to the fringe on a buckskin loincloth that was recovered from Murrah Cave (41VV351) (fig 5.16). The loincloth, placed on a bundle of Mormon tea (*Ephedra* sp.), was folded and overlain with seven pieces of red mineral pigment. Deposits have not been dated, but the loincloth was recovered from an Archaic period context (Holden 1937; Merrill 1977).

At Horseshoe Ranch Caves (41VV171) a

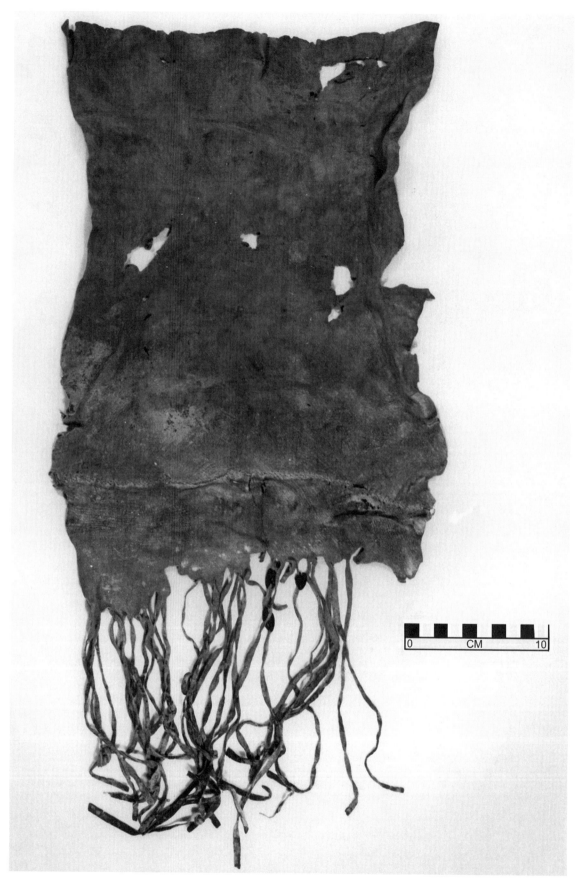

FIG. 5.16 *(Above and opposite)* Three longitudinally split mescal beans attached to the fringe of a buckskin loincloth recovered from Murrah Cave. Photograph courtesy of the Museum of Texas Tech University, Lubbock. Accession number TTU-X-2330—1.

twined bag was found covered by three layers of matting and resting on a woven rabbit fur robe or blanket. In addition to 38 mescal beans, the bag contained the following items (see fig. 5.17):

woven fiber cords
a woven package containing a flint or chert
  knife, bundles of sinew, and a small ball
  of pinkish clay
a buckskin thong
a flintknapping kit
a mussel shell
3 flint blades

5 side-scrapers
5 unworked flints
a projectile point
a flattened mano
a small terrapin carapace with holes bored
  along its outer edges
11 jackrabbit mandible halves
3 pieces of red paint stone
187 Mexican buckeye seeds (Ungnadia
  speciosa)

The bag was recovered from an Archaic period context (Martin 1933; Merrill 1977; Shafer 1986).

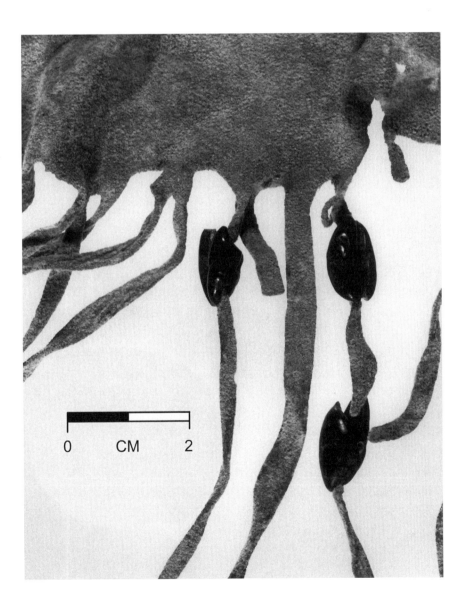

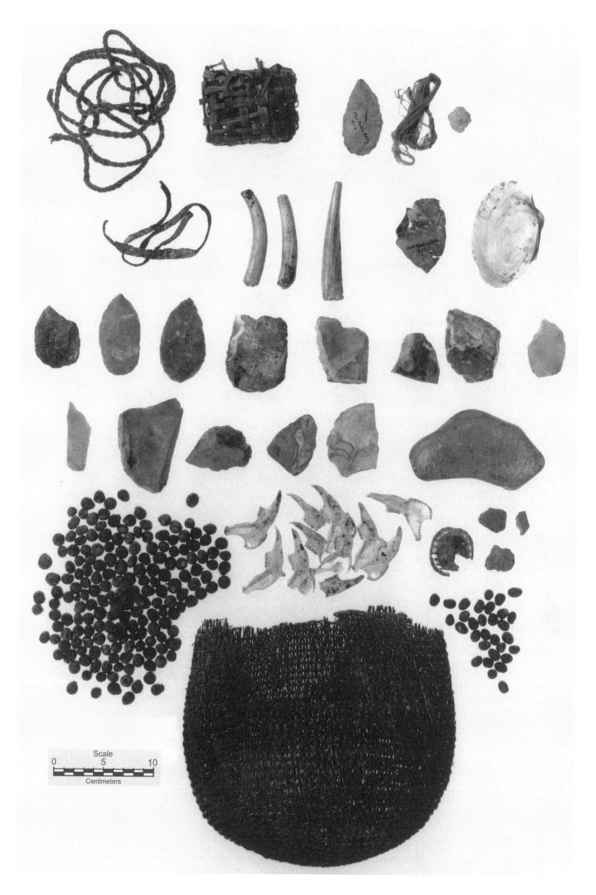

FIG. 5.17   Twine bag recovered from Horseshoe Ranch Cave containing numerous items, including mescal beans. Photograph courtesy of the Texas Archeological Research Laboratory, The University of Texas at Austin.

ETHNOGRAPHIC ACCOUNTS OF MESCALISM

Although more than thirty Native American groups are ethnographically reported to have used mescal beans, the actual association of beans in contexts associated with visions is limited. According to Hatfield et al. (1977:379), "Most, if not all of these groups used mescal beans as seed beads, which they attached to their clothing and other articles. Yet, less than half of these groups consumed mescal beans or a decoction prepared from these seeds, and the majority of the groups who did ingest mescal beans did so primarily for their emetic and purgative effects. . . . In fact, only six Native American groups are suspected to have associated the consumption of mescal beans with visionary experiences."

Although principally used as a seed bead, mescal beans have also been used medicinally and in decoctions prepared from other plants. Cheyenne are reported to have used mescal beans to prepare an eyewash; Comanche and Kickapoo utilized the seeds to cure earaches. The Mescalero and Chiricahua Apache occasionally mixed mescal beans with their corn beer. There is some evidence to show that the Coahuilteco and Hasinai Caddo consumed mescal beans in conjunction with the hallucinogenic peyote cactus (Hatfield et al. 1977). The Native American Church integrated mescal beans as items of material culture into the paraphernalia of the peyote religion during the reservation period. Today, mescal beans maintain their prominence in peyote paraphernalia (Howard 1957, 1960; La Barre 1957, 1975; Merrill 1977; Safford 1916; Schultes 1937, 1969).

MESCALISM IN THE PECOS RIVER–STYLE PICTOGRAPHS

T. N. Campbell sought an explanation for the presence of mescal bean seeds in archaeological deposits of the lower Pecos through ethno-graphic analogy. "Even a cursory examination of the Pecos River–style pictographs reveals a number of parallels to the mescal bean cult. . . . The historic cult is frequently linked with hunting and with the deer . . . and this also seems to be true of the Pecos River Focus cult" (Campbell 1958:60). He based his interpretation on parallels identified between paraphernalia utilized in the historic mescal bean cult and pictographs of the region:

1. Design elements decorating the bodies of the Pecos River–style anthropomorphs are similar to paraphernalia worn by mescal bean cult practitioners. This includes fox skins draped over the arms and wrapped about the waist of cult members, and deer tail necklaces and owl feather bracelets.

2. Anthropomorphic figures depicted with weapons in Pecos River–style rock art are analogous to men dancing with weapons during the historic mescal bean cults.

3. The stafflike object with an enlarged distal end held by the anthropomorphs in the rock art is analogous to the staff held by the leader in the ritual of at least one historic mescal bean cult.

4. The enlarged distal end of the staff held by Pecos River–style anthropomorphs, Campbell suggested, is a gourd rattle used in historic cults.

Despite subsequent archaeological research in the lower Pecos area, Campbell's interpretation has been widely cited without critical evaluation. Campbell has undoubtedly identified some interesting similarities between the pictographs and the historic mescal bean medicine society. In a previous publication (Boyd and Dering 1996), my co-author and I argued that given the presence of more powerful plants in archaeological remains, it is not reasonable to assume that inhabitants of the region were engaged solely in a mescal bean cult—if a mescal bean cult existed in the region at all. Peyote has been recovered from archaeological deposits in the lower Pecos and has been identified in four-thousand-year-old Pecos River–style pictographs. The Pecos River–style pictographs and archaeological remains of the region also contain evidence of another plant that is reported to be of great importance to shamans throughout Mexico and the American Southwest—*Datura* spp. (Boyd and Dering 1996).

Gourd Rattles, Prickly Pear Pouches, or Datura?

One motif Campbell described in relation to the historic mescal bean medicine society is the same as Motif C identified during my analysis of the Pecos River–style pictographs—anthropomorphs holding a staff-like object with an enlarged distal end (fig. 5.18). According to Campbell, the enlarged distal end may represent a gourd rattle used in the mescal bean medicine society. In *Rock Art of Texas Indians*, W. W. Newcomb (Kirkland and Newcomb 1967) reinterpreted this motif as a prickly pear pouch and concluded that more than half the anthropomorphic figures are associated with this motif. Based on morphology of the motif and supported by ethnographic and archaeological evidence, I believe this motif is neither a gourd rattle nor a prickly pear pouch but a pictographic representation of the fruit of *Datura* spp. (Boyd and Dering 1996).

THE MOTIF

The enlarged distal end of the stafflike object is most frequently depicted as an ovular or circular object with numerous spinescent protru-

FIG. 5.18 Panther Cave (41vv83). Anthropomorphs holding stafflike objects with enlarged distal ends. Scale 1cm ≈ 50cm.

sions; however, stylized versions of the motif are also present (fig. 5.19). Each of the sites included in this analysis contains this recurring motif. In the Rattlesnake Canyon pictographs, at least nine skeletonized anthropomorphs are holding the stafflike object. The White Shaman panel contains only one representation of this motif—an antlered, skeletonized anthropomorph holding the object in its left hand. At least thirteen depictions of skeletonized anthropomorphs holding the stafflike object are in the Panther Cave paintings; three are in the Mystic Shelter pictographs; and more than twenty are in the Cedar Springs panel. Morphology of the enlarged distal end with the spinescent protrusions closely resembles the fruit of datura, a powerful hallucinogenic plant associated with shamanism throughout much of North America.

BOTANY OF DATURA

Datura is a genus of the family Solanaceae, the nightshade family. Also referred to by such names as jimsonweed, devil's apple, thorn apple, and Gabriel's trumpet, *Datura* spp. has been an important medicinal and hallucinogenic plants since ancient times in both the Old and New World (Avery, Satina, and Rietsema 1959; Dobkin de Rios 1984; Harner 1973a, 1973b; Heiser 1989; Safford 1916, 1920; Schultes 1969, 1972). According to herbarium records, at least three species have been collected in or near the lower Pecos River region, *Datura stramonium, D. inoxia,* and *D. wrightii. Datura inoxia* and *D. wrightii* (fig. 5.20), both of which grow throughout the southwestern United States and northern Mexico, are closely related members of the section *Dutra. Datura stramonium* (fig. 5.21), which is in the section *Stramonium,* has a cosmopolitan distribution. All these species grow in open, disturbed areas, especially in dry washes and on river terraces throughout the lower Pecos region.

The herbaceous datura plants growing in the study area produce a white funnelform corolla that matures into a spiny fruit called a capsule. The spines, about 5 millimeters long, protrude in all directions from the fruit, giving the appearance of a spiny seed pod. The seeds are fairly large and reniform in shape with a distinctive carunculate surface. In *Datura inoxia* and *D. wrightii,* the seeds, four to five millimeters long and three to four millimeters wide, are usually a light tan color. The seeds of *Datura stramonium* are about half that size, turning black when mature (fig. 5.22).

FIG. 5.19   Datura variously depicted in the Pecos River–style rock art.

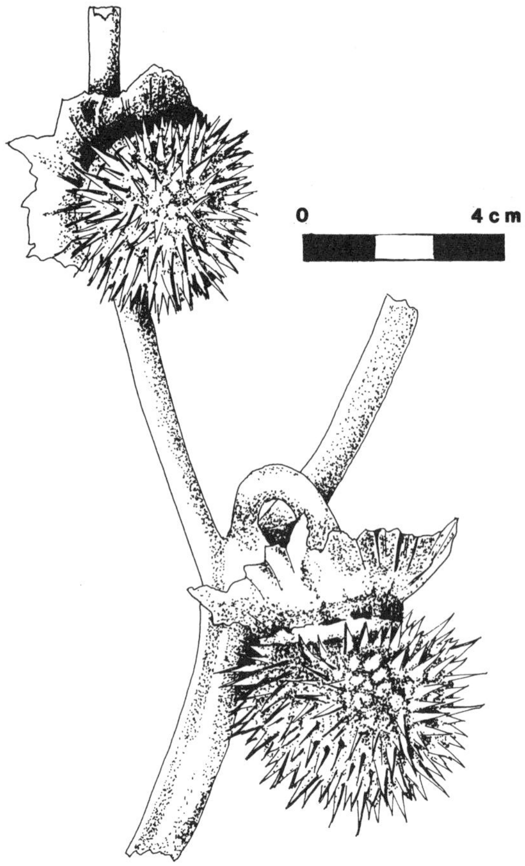

FIG. 5.20   *Datura wrightii.*

FIG. 5.21   *Datura stramonium.*

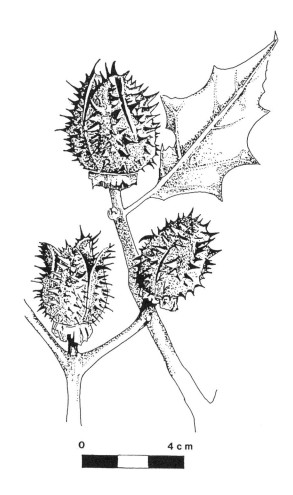

FIG. 5.22   Seed pod and seeds of *Datura wrightii*. Photograph by J. Phil Dering.

THE DATURA EXPERIENCE

Daturas produce copious alkaloids, the most predominant being the belladonna alkaloids, including atropine, hyoscine (scopolamine), and hyoscyamine. Bye, Mata, and Pimentel (1991:tables 6 and 7) have compiled a list of alkaloids extracted from *Datura lanosa* and its close relatives *D. inoxia* and *D. wrightii. Datura stramonium* apparently has a much lower alkaloid concentration than the other three species.

Although seeds contain the highest percentage of alkaloids, decoctions and powders prepared from any part of any datura plant can produce complex physiological effects when taken in toxic doses (Avery, Satina, and Rietsema 1959; Klein-Schwartz and Oderda 1984; Martinez 1969). Symptoms of low-dose datura intoxication include extreme pupil dilation, restlessness, delirium, disorientation, loss of short-term memory, high fever, dry mucous membranes, convulsions, and hallucinations.

Higher doses can cause lethargy, coma, and death. Individuals experiencing datura intoxication have been described as "hot as a hare," "red as a beet," "dry as a bone," "blind as a bat," and "mad as a hatter" (Klein-Schwartz and Oderda 1984; Kulig and Rumack 1983).

Because they are alkaloid-producing herbs, members of the Datura genus have been important constituents of pharmacopoeias around the world for centuries. Even today, datura abuse among adolescents and adults seeking the "jimsonweed high" is not uncommon (Klein-Schwartz and Oderda 1984; Mahler 1975). Many Native American cultures continue to use datura as a medicinal and ceremonial plant. According to Harner (1973b:146), the solanaceous hallucinogens are so powerful users cannot control mind and body while simultaneously performing ritual activity. Because of this and the extended period of sleep associated with high doses of datura intoxication (three to four days), Harner (1973b) argued that datura was used in vision quests rather than in shamanic rituals that would require the shaman to function in both worlds simultaneously.

IN THE HANDS OF THE SHAMAN

Ethnographic and ethnobotanical literature of the New World reveals the widespread use of datura by shamans for divination, prophecy, ecstatic initiation, ritual intoxication, diagnosis, and curing (Dobkin de Rios 1984; Furst 1976; Lewis and Elvin-Lewis 1977). Various species of datura were highly valued among pre-Columbian Mexicans as a medicinal and hallucinogenic plant (Bennet and Zingg 1935; Dibble and Anderson 1970; Pennington 1963; Zingg 1977). In the American Southwest, the Navajo, Yokut, Yuman, Paiute, Chumash, and others used the seeds, roots, and leaves in adolescent or divinatory rites (Applegate 1975; Bean and Saubel 1972; Elmore 1943; La Barre

1975; Schultes 1972; Strong 1929; Watermann 1910).

Many aboriginal tribes of southern California employed datura for its medicinal and hallucinogenic properties (Applegate 1975; Bean and Saubel 1972; Strong 1929). Among the Cahuilla Indians of California, shamans utilized the hallucinogenic properties of datura to transcend reality and take magical flights to the spirit or otherworld, flights that were considered a necessary activity. Through the use of datura, the shaman was able to journey to the spirit realm and gain information useful for his people (Barrows 1900; Bean and Saubel 1972). Among the Chumash of the central coast of California, datura was relied on for establishing contact with supernatural guardians or dream helpers, to communicate with the dead, to see into the future, to cure serious wounds and illnesses, and to counter the effects of ill omens or breaches of taboo (Applegate 1975).

In *Ethnobotany of the Zuni Indians* Matilda Coxe Stevenson relates the use of datura by Zuni rain-priests in rain-bringing rituals and divination, and by Zuni doctors to render patients unconscious during simple operations. Stevenson also points out that the flower identified as a squash blossom by other ethnographers of the Zuni is, in actuality, a datura blossom. She states that this is "an error only too pleasing to the Zuni, as the blossom of the datura is most sacred to them" (Stevenson 1915:46f). The Tarahumara Indians of northern Mexico add the roots, seeds, and leaves of datura to *tesguino,* a ceremonial offering that is consumed to induce visions. Tarahumara shaman drink a small portion of the datura mixture when making a diagnosis (Bye 1979, 1985; Pennington 1963). Among the Tarahumara, datura is considered extremely dangerous. It is believed that anyone other than a shaman who breaks the plant or pulls it up will eventually go crazy and die. Only the peyote shaman, who is armed with a plant more powerful than datura, can destroy this danger-ous weed (Bennet and Zingg 1935; Fackelman 1993).

DATURA IN ARCHAEOLOGICAL DEPOSITS

Datura is rarely identified at archaeological sites; however, in the rockshelters of the lower Pecos River region, five seeds were reported from Hinds Cave. The stratigraphic lens within which the Hinds Cave datura was found is bracketed by radiocarbon ages of 4510 ± 70 B.P. and 4990 ± 70 B.P. The seeds came from a grass mat adjacent to a hearth feature. Un-fortunately, this context does not suggest any particular use or special treatment, such as a cache (Dering 1979). Among reports from other archaeological sites that allude to cere-monial use of the plant, perhaps the most compelling is from Higgins Flat Pueblo near the San Francisco River, three miles northwest of Reserve, New Mexico. At this site, about nine hundred seeds of *Datura inoxia* (formerly called *D. meteloides*) were found on the floor of a room that yielded ceremonial objects (Cutler 1956; Cutler and Kaplan 1956; Yarnell 1959).

Although not found in a context that pro-vides insight into use of the plant, datura seed pods, datura seeds, or both have been reported from archaeological sites in Utah, New Mex-ico, and Arizona. Alice Eastwood (1893) noted that datura seed pods were frequently found in the ruins of southeastern Utah. Datura seed pod fragments were identified by Cutler and Kaplan (1956) at Montezuma Castle in central Arizona. Datura seeds were recovered from the Mattocks ruin in south-western New Mexico, Rito de los Frijoles Canyon in north-central Mexico, and Pottery Mound in northwestern New Mexico (Yarnell 1959). The strength of the pictorial represen-tation of datura in the lower Pecos, the pres-ence of datura in the archaeological deposits, and the reoccurring association of datura with

shamanism in ethnography present a forceful argument that this was an important ritual and medicinal plant utilized by shamans of the lower Pecos archaic.

Datura and Predatory Animals

In the ethnographic literature, predators—in particular, wolves and coyotes—are associated with solanaceous plants. I propose that animal counterparts for datura can also be identified in the pictographs. The physiological effects of datura intoxication provide clues to the associ-ation of these plants with canids.

EL CANCÈRBERO, THE BLACK DOG

Throughout ethnographic literature about groups in the southwestern United States and Mexico, datura is identified with witchcraft and sorcery. It is also associated with wind, which is the harbinger of illness and other mis-fortune, and canids, in particular the wolf and coyote. Many aboriginal tribes of southern California employed datura for its medicinal and hallucinogenic properties. Datura was believed to represent a powerful human sha-man with whom the aboriginal shaman could communicate. Ceremonies involving datura were conducted when there was a scarcity of water or food, or when an epidemic raged. It was an especially important component in the *toloache* (datura) boy's initiation ceremonies (Applegate 1975; Bean and Saubel 1972; Strong 1929). A decoction prepared from datura was administered to boys during initia-tion ceremonies. The *paha,* or ceremonial assistant, presided over the ceremony and was responsible for preparing and administering datura to the initiates. Coyote, one of the first and greatest shamans, was the first *paha* to pre-side over the *toloache* ceremonies (Strong 1929:108, 134).

The Chumash ingested datura to establish contact with the supernatural world. A specialist prepared and administered the datura mixture. According to a Chumash myth collected by Blackburn (1975), Coyote was the datura giver in times past when the animals were still people. The Chumash saw datura as the old woman Moymoy. Moymoy is the Chumash word for datura. Coyote, the trickster and an adept sorcerer, came into existence from Moymoy's sweat. Due to the lethal aspects of datura, it was a common ingredient in poisons made by Chumash sorcerers (Applegate 1975; Blackburn 1975).

Among the Tohono O'odham (Papago), Coyote was the messenger for the supernaturals and the giver of visions. Although Tohono O'odham hunters are reluctant to discuss the use of datura to bring about visions that assist in the deer hunt, several Tohono O'odham hunting songs indicate that the plant was used (Underhill 1969:91–93). The same is true among the Akmiel O'odham (Pima) who sing "Datura Songs" to bring success to the deer hunters (Russell 1975:300). Among the Yaqui, the coyote is perceived as having powerful *morea*, or witchcraft. Witches, said to be "from the left side," transform themselves into human coyotes. They prepare a decoction made from datura in a witching olla. When the wind blows the odor over the landscape, anyone smelling the decoction will become ill and perhaps even die (Moises, Holden Kelly, and Holden 1971:20; Painter 1986:48).

Among various Pueblo groups, coyotes are also equated with witches (Parsons 1974:193–94, 221). Animal transformation by witches is effected by donning animal pelts or by "turning over," which refers to passing through a hoop or ring. When a Hopi witch turns over, he or she becomes a coyote. Among the Hopi and Zuni, Coyote was the first witch and teacher of witchcraft. Like the Huichol, various Pueblo groups associate datura with the wind and witchcraft. Witches are believed to control weather, keeping the rain away or bringing the wind. A witch was able to bring winds by uprooting a datura plant. The winds would continue blowing until the plant's hole was filled (Parsons 1974:136n).

Although there is no mention of datura use by Zuni witches, descriptions of individuals believed to be under a witch's spell display behavior similar to that equated with datura intoxication. Stevenson describes a twelve-year-old girl suffering from severe hysteria due to witchcraft: "She rolled and tossed, pulled at her hair and throat, and threw her arms wildly about, her legs moving as violently as her arms. Her head was never quiet for a moment" (Stevenson 1904:389). Navajo witches, when assuming the form of a human wolf, often wear coyote or wolf hides. Datura was employed by Navajo witches in Frenzy Witchcraft to seduce women and for success in gambling and trading. The Prostitution Way was conducted to cure victims of Frenzy Witchcraft. Prostitution Way was considered closely linked with Coyote Way and Moth or Rabid Coyote Way (Kluckhohn 1944:230). During the ceremony, singers of the Prostitution Way chant supervised an individual's use of datura for purposes of divination. The antidote for the diagnostician was a plant called "deer eye" (Kluckhohn 1944:176).

In *Mitobotánica Zapoteca*, Blas Pablo Reko (1945:104) identified the word for datura in the Zapotec language as *Xolo* or *Xholo*. The association of datura with canids is clear in his definition for the Zapotec term:

Xolotl (azt.), el cancérbero. Nombre sugestivo del mito de la mandrágora, cuya raíz ha de ser arrancada por un perro negro (xolotl). Aquí el toloáche mexicano sustituye a la mandrágora europea, porque los dos son drogas obnubilantes. (Xolotl, the three-headed dog which guards the gate of the nether world. Suggestive name for the mandrake myth, whose root is to be pulled out by a black dog [Xolotl].

Here the Mexican datura substitutes the European mandrake, because both are drugs that confuse the nervous system [translation by C. E. Boyd].)

Zapotec witches were most frequently reported to take the form of a dog. Parsons (1936) relates several tales in which the witch animal is a dog. One particular tale told by a Zapotec man, especially illustrative of the witch/dog relationship, is about a boy who fell in love with a girl. The girl persuaded the lovesick boy to go for a walk with her in the evening. While on their walk, she rubbed some grease on his hands and told him to roll over. He did so, and felt himself being transformed into a black dog, *xolotl*. The girl did the same to herself and became a black bitch. The bitch left the dog, telling him to wait for her while she went to talk to several other witches that were also dogs. After the boy and girl changed back into people, the boy beat the girl for what she did to him. He awakened ill the next day and eventually died (Parsons 1936:133).

Associations between datura, witches or sorcerers, the wind, and the canids is perhaps most evident among the Huichol Indians of northern Mexico. Wolf shamanism and transformation among the Huichol is both symbolically and practically associated with three closely related solanaceous plants—*Datura* spp., *Solandra* spp., and *Brugmansia* spp. The Huichol incorporate these plants into the collective symbolism of the psychotropic god-plant Kiéri. Although the *Solandra* spp. is considered to represent the "good" Kiéri and datura the "crazy" Kiéri or Kieritsa, the tropane alkaloids contained in both solanaceous plants produce similar pharmacological effects (Evans 1979). The effects of Kiéri "are said to be far stronger than those of peyote and said to be accompanied by sickness and possible blindness. The plant is said to be able to make an individual crazy or even kill him. . . . It is

also said to produce no visual signs like peyote but instead rather frightening visions of 'snakes and wolves and venomous creatures'"(Knab 1977:85).

Kiéri is believed to be "born from the wind, on the wind, an evil wind" (Furst and Myerhoff 1966:8). He is equated with the animals of sorcery and shamanic power, in particular canids—the coyote and wolf. Furst and Myerhoff (1966) see connections between Aztec cosmology, the characterization of Kiéri as the "Tree of the Wind," and his association with the wolf. They noted, "In the Florentine Codex, Sahagún tells us that those born under the sign of *Ce Ehecatl,* One Wind, are destined to become sorcerers. If they are nobility, they can become werewolves and also take on other forms at will" (Furst and Myerhoff 1966:33).

Singing shamans would eat *yerba de lobo* (herb of the wolf) five times in order to make themselves into wolves, and once in that form, they would hunt deer (Lumholtz 1902:261). Susan Eger Valadez (1996:287) proposed that the *yerba de lobo* referenced by Lumholtz may be the solanaceous wolf-kiéri, which is an integral component of Huichol wolf shamanism and wolf transformation. According to Valadez's informant Ulu Temay, "One eats the wolf-kiéri in order to have an exhibition, a vision, of what it will be like to become a wolf" (Valadez 1996:287). As with the Hopi and Zapotec, transformation into one of the canids involves "turning over." The individual "does five turns and then turns into a wolf" (Valadez 1996:289).

LYCANTHROPY: THE DATURA HIGH

Lycanthropy, the belief that one can change into a wolf or a similar predator, is frequently associated with solanaceous hallucinogens such as datura. The *Datura* spp. produce copious alkaloids, primarily the belladonna alkaloids, including atropine, hyoscine (scopolamine), and hyoscyamine. Decoctions and powders prepared from any part of any of the datura plant produce complex physiological effects when taken in toxic doses (Avery, Satina, and Rietsema 1959; Klein-Schwartz and Oderda 1984; Mahler 1975; Martinez 1969). Ointments prepared from the plant can produce the same physiological effects because atropine can be absorbed through the skin (Cooper 1791; Klein-Schwartz and Oderda 1984). "Those labouring under lycanthropia go out during the night imitating wolves in all things and lingering about sepulchers until morning. You may recognize such persons by these marks: they are pale, their vision feeble, their eyes dry, tongue very dry, and the flow of the saliva stopped; but they are thirsty, and their legs have incurable ulcerations from frequent falls. Such are the marks of the disease" (Adams, cited in Harner 1973b:141).

The "marks of the disease" of lycanthropy, described above, closely resemble those reported for clinical effects of datura poisoning (Harner 1973b:141). Symptomatology of low-dose datura intoxication includes extreme pupil dilation, restlessness, delirium, disorientation, loss of short-term memory, high fever, dry mucous membranes, convulsions, and hallucinations. Severe photophobia resulting from pupil dilation is repeatedly associated with datura intoxication. A young girl suffering from datura poisoning experienced such an extreme degree of pupil dilation that she was able to see clearly at night, but was nearly blinded by the light of day (Cooper 1791). Pupil dilation reportedly persists for several days after the ingestion of datura seeds (Klein-Schwartz and Oderda 1984).

Combative and aggressive behavior is typical of individuals experiencing datura intoxication. The symptoms have been described as similar to those of rabies, whereby a patient reportedly bites, strikes, and screams, wildly throwing his arms about, picking and grasping at imaginary objects. Individuals experience

extreme thirst; however, the sight of water "throws him into a spasm, foaming at the mouth and other symptoms similar to those of hydrophobia" (Millspaugh 1974:502). Ireland (1817) quoted a report by Dr. Haygarth in a Bath newspaper that describes the behavior of children following the consumption of *Datura stramonium* seeds. The children "were seized with very violent convulsions and vomiting; an alarming pain in the head, stomach, and bowels: the latter with blindness, and a kind of madness; biting, scratching, shrieking, laughing, and crying, in a frightful manner" (Ireland 1817:11).

The same alkaloids that have been chemically identified in the genus Datura have also been identified in related solanaceous plants such as *Atropa belladonna* (belladonna) and *Mandragora officinarum* (mandrake). These plants have a long history of use in sorcery and witchcraft, and generate physiological effects similar to datura. Following the ingestion or absorption of the atropine and scopolamine alkaloids contained in the plants, witches enter a hallucinatory state during which they journey to a rendevous with spirits and demons. While in this state, they are reported to experience the hallucination of being transformed into a predatory animal, in particular the wolf. This transformation was facilitated through the tactile suggestions produced by wearing wolf skins or wolf skin girdles (Harner 1973b; Verstegan 1628). "The Were-Wolues are certayne Sorcerers, who having annoynted their bodies, with an Oyntment which they make by the instinct of the Divell: And putting on a certayne Inchaunted Girdle, doe not onely unto the view of others, seeme as Wolues, but to their owne thinking have both the Shape, and the Nature of Wolues, so long as they weare the sayd girdle: And they doe dispose themselves as very Wolues, in wourrying, and killing, and most of Humane Creatures" (Verstegan 1628:237). The solanaceous plant ointment was used in experiencing witches' flight and in metamorphosing into a werewolf. The expectations and desires of the subject and the cues in his or her immediate environment strongly affect the nature of the hallucinatory experience (Harner 1973b).

CANID/DATURA RELATIONSHIP

The physiological effects associated with datura intoxication illuminate the association of datura and canids. The symptomatology of datura intoxication is repeatedly equated with the behavior of canid predators. Individuals experiencing datura intoxication are described as restless and aggressive, and display symptoms of hydrophobia (rabies), such as extreme thirst, foaming at the mouth, biting, and striking. Intoxicated individuals not only appear to others to behave as predatory animals of the night but also believe themselves to be transformed into such animals. The hallucinosis is completed by the sensation of the growing of feathers and hair (Hesse 1946). The sensation of becoming a predatory animal evoked by the solanaceae hallucinogens is so strong that individuals have been reported to physically attack a number of persons on various occasions, biting them with their teeth, killing them, and even eating parts of their bodies (Harner 1973b). Another notable effect of datura intoxication is the ability to see clearly at night due to pupil dilation. These are characteristics equated with nocturnal canids, such as the coyote and the wolf. Datura is also nocturnal, with the blossoms of the plant opening during the night and closing after sunrise.

OTHER SOLANACEOUS PREDATORS

Felines have also been associated with solanaceous plants. Johannes Wilbert (1987) identified a close relationship between South American tobacco shamanism and the jaguar. Tobacco-producing plants are derived from

the genus *Nicotiana,* which like *Datura* spp. is a member of the nightshade family. The mind-altering effect of nicotine lies at the core of tobacco shamanism and shaman/jaguar transformation. Several tobacco-related characteristics of a tobacco shaman likened him to the jaguar, such as acuteness of vision, night vision, wakefulness, raspy voice, furred or rough tongue, pungent body odor, and aggressive behavior. According to Wilbert (1987:197), the "nicotine-associated physiological, neuropsychological, and cultural factors seem to constitute the essential ingredients of were-jaguar shamanism in South America."

Predators in the Pictographs

The two predators depicted in the pictographs of the lower Pecos are canids and felines. Turpin (1994) suggested that the abundant representation of felines in the art is indicative of a were-cougar theme in the Pecos River–style pictographs. She proposed that anthropomorphic figures with cat ears, claws, striped underbelly, and blank faces are depictions of a human-feline composite in which the mountain lion serves as the shaman's animal familiar (fig. 5.23). In light of Wilbert's (1987) research, Turpin's (1994) identification of a were-cougar theme in the Pecos River–style rock art is intriguing. Although tobacco has not yet been identified in the archaeological deposits, its prevalent use by Native American groups is well documented. Although further research is warranted, I believe Turpin's identification of a were-cougar theme in the art is accurate and may provide insight into the presence of tobacco shamanism in the lower Pecos.

The second predator identified in the pictographs of the lower Pecos River region is a canid, perhaps a coyote or wolf. Although not frequently represented, canids have been identified in the Pecos River–, Red Linear–, and

FIG. 5.23 Panther Cave (41vv83), Seminole Canyon.
Were-cougar at Panther Cave as identified by Turpin (1994).
Photograph by James Harrison III.

Red Monochrome–style art. At Fate Bell annex, a polychrome Pecos River–style anthropomorph is holding datura in the left hand with an unidentified quadruped—perhaps a canid—at the right arm (fig. 5.24). A second quadruped is adjacent to the left side of the anthropomorph. At Painted Canyon, Red Monochrome–style images line the wall of a rock shelter (41vv78). These images are superimposed over the top of Pecos River–style rock art that, before the addition of the more recent pictographs, was almost entirely abraded by repeated flooding of the shelter. The canine depicted in this panel is facing left and is located just behind the hindquarters of a large deer, which is facing the opposite direction (see fig. 5.14). The body of the deer is decorated with a design that strongly resembles the Huichol symbol for peyote.

The appearance of canids increases in the Red Linear style. The Pressa Canyon Red Linear site (41vv201) provides an excellent example of the association of canids with datura (fig. 5.25). Below a vertical row of

eleven rigid, spiny-headed stick figures with erect phalli is a horizontal row of at least ten canids. To the left of these figures is the depiction of a plant emerging from the head of a Red Linear anthropomorph. Two canids are associated with this plant: one is positioned on a stem; the other is hanging upside down from another stem (fig. 5.26). This Red Linear image is similar to a datura plant depiction in a Huichol yarn painting that relates the mythic battle between Kauyumári (Sacred Deer Person) and Crazy Kiéri (Datura Person) (fig. 5.27). In yarn paintings, depictions of Kiéri are frequently associated with wolves, coyotes, or foxes (fig. 5.28). The canid, an animal familiar of Kiéri, is depicted to the left of the datura plant illustrated in the yarn painting. Crazy Kiéri is depicted with a spiny head; Kauyumári, with antlers. The Red Linear depiction of the deer with dots on the antler tines and impaled dots mentioned earlier in this chapter, as well as other deer figures and anthropomorphs, are located approximately fourteen meters to the left of the panel

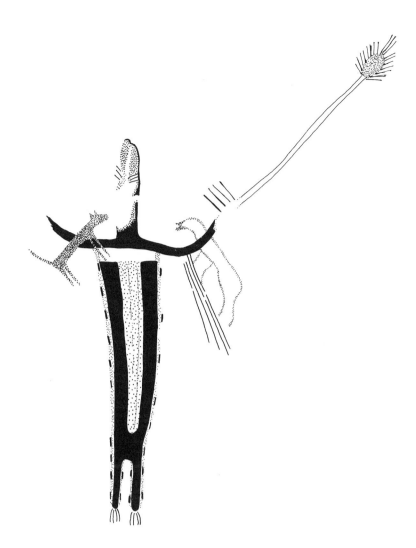

FIG. 5.24 Fate Bell Annex (41vv74).
Quadrupeds associated with
anthropomorph holding datura.
Scale 1cm ≈ 13cm.

FIG. 5.25 Pressa Canyon Red Linear site
(41vv201). Spiny-headed
anthropomorph associated
with a row of canids. This panel
is located approximately 14
meters to the right of the panel
illustrated in FIG. 5.11.
Scale 1cm ≈ 2.5cm.

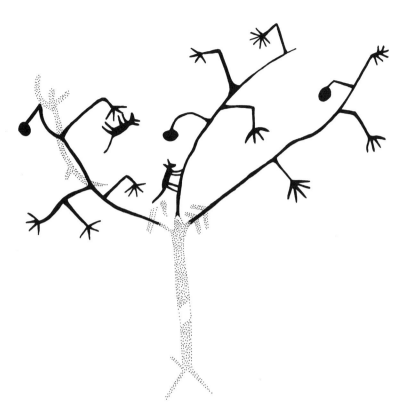

FIG. 5.26 Pressa Canyon Red Linear site (41vv201). Plantlike image associated with canids. Scale 1 cm ≈ 2.5 cm.

described above. None of the anthropomorphs associated with the deer have the spiny heads of those associated with the plant.

In the pictographs, the spiny-headed stick figures, the canids, the plant resembling datura, and the depiction of canids both on the plant and below the spiny-headed stick figures illustrate the metaphorical relationship between canids and datura. Although datura has not been identified in the Red Monochrome–style art, the coyote illustrated in an opposing fashion to the peyote/deer in the Painted Canyon rock shelter may suggest the datura/ coyote relationship.

Contrary Characters

In the myths and folktales of groups in northern Mexico and the American Southwest, an antagonistic relationship is illustrated between the plants peyote and datura, their animal counterparts deer and coyote, and the shamans associated with each. For example, the

Tarahumara consider datura to be extremely dangerous. It is believed that anyone who breaks a plant or pulls one up will eventually go crazy and die. Only the peyote shaman, being protected by a plant more powerful than datura, can safely destroy this dangerous weed (Bennett and Zingg 1935; Fackelmann 1993). Peyote has been reportedly used as antiwitch medicine at Taos Pueblo (Parsons 1974:13) and as an antidote to datura poisoning by the Huichols (Lumholtz 1902; Myerhoff 1974) and the Tarahumara (Bennett and Zingg 1935). The Navajo use a plant referred to as "deer eye" as an antidote for datura (Kluckholn 1944).

The most explicit example of an antithetical relationship between the two hallucinogens and their animal counterparts is provided in a Huichol myth about a contest between Kauyumári, who is Deer and whose ally and alter ego is peyote *(Lophophora williamsii),* and his adversary the malevolent sorcerer Crazy Kiéri, the personification of *Datura inoxia.* Through his intoxicating juices and the use of sorcery,

FIG. 5.27 Huichol yarn painting by Ramón Medina illustrating Datura Person tempting a woman with the datura plant. Datura Person is located in the top left portion of the painting. Redrawn from Furst and Myerhoff (1966).

FIG. 5.28 Huichol yarn painting by Ramón Medina illustrating the battle between Datura Person *(bottom right)* and Sacred Deer Person *(center)*. Datura Person is identified with the fox *(upper left)*, the animal of sorcery and death. Redrawn from Furst and Myerhoff (1966).

Crazy Kiéri attempts to lure the Huichol away from using peyote to using datura instead. In an effort to save his people from the evil ways of datura, the horned culture-hero Kauyumári vanquishes Crazy Kiéri and his followers with the aid of peyote.

Furst and Myerhoff (1966:8n) noted: "It is not impossible that the two protagonists whose struggle is recorded in this myth cycle are historical figures, perhaps the leaders of two rival cults." If this is the case, Coyote, a "mythical" character encountered in northern Mexico and the American Southwest, may actually be a historical figure—a shaman whose plant of choice was datura. The physiological effects of the powerful plant caused the shaman to behave like and become transformed into his animal counterpart, the coyote. I propose, however, that Coyote is not a historical figure in the literal sense (a single shaman), but rather that Coyote is the solanaceous plant that facilitates canid transformation.

The antagonistic relationship between peyote shamans and datura shamans, I believe, has its origins in the distinctive natural history of the plants and their animal counterparts. Tensions observed and experienced in the physical realm between deer and coyote and between the physiological effects of peyote and datura intoxication are manifested as metaphysical battles between good and evil and communicated by shaman/artists via myths, folklore, and art.

Art, Artists, and Politics

Noting that when one faith displaces another, the losing side is often banished to the realm of sorcery and witchcraft, Furst (Schaefer and Furst 1996:234) asked: "Could the solanaceous 'Kiéri cult' and its present association with sorcery be a remnant of a greater Southwestern pre-peyote substratum?" Identification

of the peyote/deer and datura/canid association in the four-thousand-year-old Pecos River–style rock art of the lower Pecos demonstrates considerable antiquity for both "cults." However, in the Pecos River–style art, datura depictions are more abundant than imagery associated with peyotism. In this study, there were at least five times as many anthropomorphs depicted with datura than with peyote. Interestingly, in some cases, such as at the White Shaman site antlered anthropomorphs with peyote on their antler tines are depicted holding datura (see fig. 4.3). Not until the Red Linear–style pictographs (1280–1150 B.P..) do we see a separation of deer/peyote and coyote/datura in the art. Furst's question is an intriguing one, which the rock art and archaeology of the lower Pecos may help answer.

Plant/animal associations identified in lower Pecos art may represent the earliest depictions of the deer as a culture hero, provider of peyote and intermediary between shamans and deities. Similarly, these pictographs may be the earliest depictions of Coyote, the first *paha* to administer datura, messenger for the supernaturals and giver of visions. Further, identification of both characters in the art, especially in the more recent Red Monochrome and Red Linear imagery, may reflect the emergence of a struggle for power between peyote and datura shamans. The shaman/artists of the lower Pecos may have been manipulating the art to serve specific political purposes—peyote shamans and datura shamans negotiating social relations and status through art.

Dowson (1998) and Lewis-Williams (1995a) have suggested that shaman/artists actively used art in such negotiations. Dowson has identified power struggles between San shamans as represented in the rock art of South Africa and has argued that these power struggles "were negotiated (not just reflected) in the art. The art, produced by shamans, became active and instrumental in forging new social relations that developed out of these power struggles" (Dowson 1998:338). Biesele (1983) noted that San trance experiences are regarded as unique, truthful, and important messages from the spiritual realm that can be obtained only through trancing. It was the role of the shaman/artist to convey these messages from the otherworld to people of the real world. The San rock paintings were one way shamans communicated this information. Among the Plains Indians of North America, Irwin (1994) demonstrated that mythic discourse and the visual arts served essential roles in sharing the dream experience with members of society.

Existing social and religious identities were reinforced or transformed and new ones were created through the manipulation of rock art in the lower Pecos. Tensions experienced in the physical realm were confronted and negotiated in the metaphysical realm; the battles, victories, and defeats were portrayed in the art. Because of the truth-value accorded the paintings, manipulation of the imagery by the shaman/artist was akin to manipulating the universe—the universe of the lower Pecos foragers.

Six

UNVEILING THE WORK OF ART

All visionary art is sacred and more than decorative or purely aesthetic. . . .
It is not art for the sake of art; it is an expression of the sacred that has an impact
and an instrumental effect on the awareness and actions of the individual or group.

L. IRWIN, *The Dream Seekers: Native American Visionary Traditions of the Great Plains*

Explaining Prehistoric Rock Art

Although archaeological research in the lower Pecos has produced an especially rich collection of material culture, many questions regarding hunter-gatherer lifeways and belief systems remain unanswered. Researchers have neglected to consider a vast data resource, uniquely accessible facts of prehistory contained in the rock art of the region. The failure to recognize the contribution of rock art to the reconstruction of prehistory, I believe, was due in part to Western conceptions of art as superfluous, decorative, and nonutilitarian. Rock art, therefore, was not integrated with other archaeological data and subjected to analogous methods of analysis. Unlike tools made of stone, wood, and fiber, rock art was not considered an integral part of hunter-gatherer adaptation—it was not useful, only beautiful. However, the recognized role of

visual imagery in many non-Western societies is vastly different from ours (see chap. 2). Images are considered sources of power; they are potent and important. An art object is valued in terms of what it can do, socially and spiritually, rather than what it looks like. The art *works*—it *performs*.

The translation of information from ethnographic literature to the archaeological record cannot be direct, and we cannot assume that the role of art in prehistory was the same as it is today in non-Western societies. However, by analyzing rock art along with other archaeological data, we can begin to recognize the myriad ways in which rock art was ingrained within every aspect of the lower Pecos socio-cultural systems during the Archaic period.

In my research, I have addressed the rock art of the lower Pecos as an archaeological feature studied within the broader contexts of archaeological sites and region. I began by conducting a feature analysis of the rock art in order to identify patterns in the archaeological record. Analysis revealed patterns in the geographic distribution of pictographic elements and motifs—recurring themes in the rock art consisting of two or more pictographic elements. My review of the literature revealed ethnographic motifs that were similar to pictographic motifs identified during the feature analysis. The patterns embodied in the art and ethnography were used to formulate hypotheses for three rock art motifs. These hypotheses were tested against the lower Pecos material record and evaluated in relation to well-documented neuroscience research associated with altered states of consciousness. All resulting data were considered within the context of the social and biophysical environment of the region. Results of this research are summarized in figures 6.1–6.3.

Pecos River–style rock art is generally accepted as shamanic art. Consequently, it should come as no surprise that the rock art contains images of shamanic flight, animal spirit helpers, and other universal aspects of shamanism. Labeling the art as shamanic, however, does little, if anything, to expand our knowledge of human behavior. Hunter-gatherers, past and present, live under specific social and environmental conditions that generate considerable behavioral variability within societies that practice shamanism. Shamanism, after all, is not a religion—it is a religious configuration within which one can see shamanic practice and symbolism side by side with or incorporated into other traditions (Wright 1989).

As archaeologists, our goal is not only to reconstruct the past, that is, identify the rock paintings as shamanic art, but also to explain the art in the broader context within which it was produced—biophysical and social.

Rock Art as Technology

The Pecos River–style rock art contains numerous depictions of atlatls, rabbit sticks, spears, and feathered darts—items that are readily accepted as part of the technological systems employed by the inhabitants of the region during the Archaic period. I argue, however, that the rock art not only contains imagery reflecting prehistoric technology but also is a form of technology in and of itself.

COMMUNICATION

Technology is defined as the application of knowledge for practical ends. I suggest that the lower Pecos rock art was an integral part of the technological system used by hunter-gatherer inhabitants of the region. The work performed by both the art and the artist should be viewed as totally practical in effect. The rock art was used to indirectly communicate information necessary for successful exploitation of the hunting and gathering niche—information regarding the biophysical and social environment, animal behavior, and ecological relationships (see chap. 4). Produced by members of an egalitarian society within which direct instruction or order-giving was considered inappropriate, the rock art was a vehicle through which important information and instruction could be disseminated to the community without threatening autonomy.

SUBSISTENCE

Important subsistence information regarding the biophysical environment and animal behavior is incorporated into the rock art imagery. For example, Motif B, the peyote-deer motif (see fig. 6.2), contains information regarding real-world ecological relationships—the effects of rainfall on deer movement; rainfall and wild plant food availability; and the availability of an important medicine and sacrament, the peyote cactus. The relationship

FIG. 6.1   Motif A: The Otherworld Journey

Pictographic Elements

- Crenelated arch has opening in the center of the arch.
- Skeletonized anthropomorphic figure is located either above, below, or behind the arch.
- Animals or animal attributes are associated with the skeletonized anthropomorph.

Ethnographic Elements

- Shamans journey to the supernatural realm or otherworld (land of the dead) to confront supernatural forces on behalf of their group.
- Shamanic journeys to the otherworld involve entering altered states of consciousness (ASC).
- Communication with or access to the otherworld is through a serpent that separates the temporal world from the otherworld.
- Caves serve as sacred portals or passageways for the shamans on their journey to the otherworld.
- Tutelary animals or animal familiars enable the shaman to forsake the human condition and be reborn into the otherworld in animal form.
- Journeys to the otherworld involve ritual death, which can include dismemberment, "killing" with arrows, and skeletonization.

Hypothesis

When found in association, elements of Motif A are graphic representations of shamanic journeys to the otherworld.

Testing the Hypothesis

COGNITIVE NEUROSCIENCE AND ALTERED STATES OF CONSCIOUSNESS

- The crenelated arch: Individuals entering an ASC frequently report seeing undulating lines often described as snakes.
- The opening in the arch: In deep ASC individuals report a tunnel or vortex surrounding and engulfing them; at the end of the vortex is a bright light or hole; individuals report the sensation of either falling into or flying through the hole in the vortex.
- Skeletonization: Individuals in deep ASC report that their limbs seem to become detached from their bodies.
- Animals and animal attributes: In deep ASC individuals report encountering animals and becoming transformed into animals.

ARCHAEOLOGY

- Land of the dead: Disposal of the dead in the lower Pecos often involved placing the body in a vertical or horizontal shaft cave.
- The crenelated arch: The arch is formed by the walls of the vertical and horizontal shaft cave; it is the body of the serpent and the vortex or tunnel.
- The opening in the arch: The opening in the earth's surface at the cave's entrance is the opening in the arch; it is the mouth of the serpent, the portal to the otherworld, and the light at the end of the tunnel.

Conclusion

The pictographic elements of Motif A record the shamanic journey achieved during altered states of consciousness. Crenelated arches represent the serpent as the gateway or vehicle to the otherworld; the opening in the arch represents the portal through which the shaman enters the otherworld. Animals and animal attributes associated with the skeletonized anthropomorph represent the shaman's animal familiar. Skeletonization is used to indicate that the shaman has experienced ritual death and been reborn into the otherworld.

FIG. 6.2   Motif B: Peyotism

Pictographic Elements

- Impaled deer and impaled dots are associated with antlered anthropomorphs whose antler tines are decorated with black dots.

Ethnographic Elements

- Deer and peyote are woven into one inseparable sacred symbol—deer is peyote and peyote is deer.
- Sacred Deer Person brought peyote on his antler tines; wherever the deer steps, peyote will grow in its tracks.
- The Huichol make a pilgrimage to hunt the peyote/deer; once the shaman locates the peyote/deer, he shoots it with an arrow.
- Peyote "buttons" are attached to the tines of the deer antlers carried by shamans on the peyote pilgrimage.
- The peyote/deer is sacrificed to bring rain.

Hypothesis

A metaphorical relationship between deer and peyote existed during the lower Pecos Archaic.

Testing the Hypothesis

COGNITIVE NEUROSCIENCE AND PEYOTE INTOXICATION

- Individuals taking peyote claim to be as agile as deer; they have been described as "jumping like deer."
- Eating peyote allays thirst and suppresses appetite.

ECOLOGY AND ANIMAL BEHAVIOR

- Rain brings deer: In the Chihuahuan Desert, deer travel rapidly to areas where it has recently rained to seek fresh forage.
- Rain brings peyote: During drought conditions, peyote shrinks beneath the surface of the ground and becomes difficult to find; immediately after rainfall, peyote swells, becoming visible on the surface of the ground.

LOWER PECOS SUBSISTENCE

- Rain increases availability of plant foods; rainfall increases the production of desert ephemerals and triggers leafing and flowering of important forage and fruit-bearing shrubs.
- Rainfall increases the availability of game; deer follow the rain.

ARCHAEOLOGY

- Peyote has been recovered from deposits at Shumla Caves in the lower Pecos.
- Various items of material culture recovered from excavations in the lower Pecos are similar to paraphernalia used in peyote ceremonies.
- Motif B has been identified at several other sites in the region.
- The pictographic panel at the White Shaman site (41VV124) contains additional elements associated with the Huichol peyote pilgrimage.

Conclusion

A metaphorical relationship between deer and peyote existed in the lower Pecos during the Archaic period. When found in association, impaled deer, impaled dots, and dots on deer antler tines represent peyote. The peyote/deer was sacrificed to bring rain, thereby increasing the availability of three important resources—deer, wild plant foods, and peyote.

FIG. 6.3   Motif C: Datura Shamanism

Pictographic Elements

- Anthropomorphic figures are holding stafflike objects with enlarged, usually spinescent, distal ends.

Ethnographic Elements

- Datura is one of the most important medicinal and hallucinogenic plants used since ancient times in both the Old and New World.
- Datura is used by shamans for the purpose of divination, prophecy, ecstatic initiation, ritual intoxication, diagnosis, and curing.
- Datura is highly valued as a medicinal and hallucinogenic plant and is used to transcend reality and take magical flights.
- Datura is associated with predatory animals, particularly the canids, and is equated with witchcraft and sorcery.

Botany

- Three species of *Datura* spp. grow in the lower Pecos River region.
- Spiny *Datura* spp. seed pods resemble the enlarged distal end of the stafflike object depicted in Motif B.
- All parts of *Datura* spp. plants produce copious alkaloids; the seeds contain the highest percentage of alkaloids.

Hypothesis

The enlarged distal end of the stafflike object held by anthropomorphic figures represents datura in the hands of shamans.

Testing the Hypothesis

COGNITIVE NEUROSCIENCE AND DATURA INTOXICATION

- Symptomatology of low-dose datura intoxication includes extreme pupil dilation, restlessness, delirium, loss of short-term memory, high fever, dry mucous membranes, hydrophobia, aggressive behavior, convulsions, and hallucinations.
- High doses can cause lethargy, coma, and death.
- Individuals intoxicated with datura report the sensation of being transformed into a wolf.
- Such individuals are described as behaving like a rabid dog—growling, biting, and foaming at the mouth.

ARCHAEOLOGY

- Seeds have been identified in Archaic deposits from Hind's Cave, a lower Pecos rockshelter.
- Seeds and seed pods have been reported from archaeological sites throughout the American Southwest.
- At Higgins Flat Pueblo in New Mexico, 900 seeds were found on the floor of a room that yielded ceremonial objects.
- Motif C appears in pictographs throughout the region.
- Motif C and other pictographic elements resembling the datura plant are found in association with a canidlike animal at the Pressa Canyon Red Linear Site and Fate Bell Annex.

Conclusion

Datura spp. was an important medicinal and hallucinogenic plant used by magico-religious practitioners during the lower Pecos Archaic period. When found in association with anthropomorphic figures, the stafflike object with the enlarged distal end represents datura.

between rain, deer, and peyote was integrated into the belief system and rituals conducted by people of the lower Pecos Archaic. Their rock art reflects a metaphorical relationship between deer and peyote—deer was peyote and peyote was deer. In Huichol mythology, the peyote/deer was sacrificed to bring rain. In the lower Pecos during the Archaic period, both rain and deer were scarce resources; therefore, the purpose of the ritual identified in the art may also have been to bring rain, which in turn brought deer, peyote, and plant foods (see chap. 5).

Just because this ecological relationship was integrated into the rituals and belief system of the lower Pecos Archaic, it should not detract from the fact that it contains practical and necessary instruction for successful exploitation of the environment. What is important here is not whether the sacrifice of the peyote/deer actually brought rain, but that it established the relationship between rainfall and the arrival of deer, wild plant foods, and peyote. This type of information would have been important in making decisions regarding band mobility—determining when and where to move.

Peyote and datura may also have been utilized to increase hunting prowess. The Machiguenga of Peru consume a variety of sedges containing alkaloids that act as a physical and mental stimulant to improve their aim and concentration while hunting (Eliot 1998). Alkaloids in peyote increase stamina, induce mental exhilaration, and heighten senses (E. Anderson 1996), all physiological effects that could be beneficial to a hunter. Machiguenga men use sedge liquid as eyedrops to improve their vision (Eliot 1998). Datura could have been used to improve vision for night hunting. When a liquid is prepared from datura and placed in the eyes, it causes extreme pupil dilation and makes it possible to see clearly at night, yet be blinded in daylight.

MEDICAL BOTANY

Two plants identified in archaeological deposits of the lower Pecos—peyote (Lophophora williamsii) and Datura spp.—have been determined to possess medicinal and hallucinogenic properties. The finding of these plants in site deposits has generated speculation regarding their use as medicines and in ritual. Motifs B and C contain information regarding the use of these plants as sacrament, medicine, and a bridge to the otherworld (see figs. 6.2 and 6.3).

As a medicine, peyote has been used during childbirth and to treat tuberculosis, pneumonia, rheumatism, scarlet fever, snake bites, broken bones, as well as other diseases and ailments. Scientists have identified within peyote an antibiotic substance that has been demonstrated to have a definite in vitro antiseptic action against a wide variety of microorganisms. Datura is also associated with medicinal purposes and has been ethnographically reported as a treatment for hydrophobia (rabies), sprained limbs, bone fractures, asthma, rattlesnake and tarantula bites, gout, and piles. It has also been used to render patients unconscious during surgery. Today, Datura spp. alkaloids are important constituents in numerous Western medicines.

The psychoactive properties of peyote and datura were employed by lower Pecos shamans to enter altered states of consciousness. Both these plants contain powerful alkaloids capable of producing vivid auditory, tactile, olfactory, and visual hallucinations. In the ethnographic literature, peyote and datura are the two plants most commonly associated with shamanism and altered states. Peyote and datura were utilized by shamans during the lower Pecos both for their medicinal and their psychoactive properties.

Rock Art and Social Relations

One of the major theses of this book is that both the art and artist perform active roles in the creation, maintenance, and transformation of social relations and religious identities. Shaman/artists are cognizant of the conditions necessary for the reproduction of society and, as such, create as well as participate in their community through the production of visual imagery.

TERRITORY AND PROPERTY RIGHTS

One of the patterns identified during the formal analysis of the art is the geographic distribution of specific pictographic elements. The identification of particular pictographic elements associated with specific geographical regions—such as feather hipclusters in the rock art of Seminole and Painted Canyons, and rabbit-eared anthropomorphs in Rattlesnake Canyon and canyons to west of the Pecos River—suggest that the rock art may have been used to delineate territories and designate property rights. Although more data are needed before this can be empirically tested, it appears that lower Pecos rock art will provide researchers with the information necessary to determine issues regarding hunter-gatherer territoriality and property rights.

TRANSLATING INDIVIDUAL EXPERIENCE INTO SHARED EXPERIENCE

Art has an active role in day-to-day social relations, communicating important information regarded by members of the community as unique messages from the supernatural realm. The artist, although constrained to some degree by tradition, communicates new information to the community through art and, at the same time, reinforces existing knowledge.

Both art and artist contribute to religious unity within an egalitarian community, transforming individual religious revelation or experience into culturally shared images. An interweaving of tradition and creativity keeps the society itself alive; individuals experience their own lives as contributions to shared reality (Biesele 1983).

The lower Pecos otherworld journey motif (see fig. 6.1) is an example of the transformation of the individual experience into the shared experience. The motif works to communicate this experience to the members of society and, at the same time, shapes and facilitates the trance experience of initiate shamans. The motif communicates not only "mythical" or metaphysical information regarding the structure of the cosmos but also factual neurological data regarding the trance experience.

RESTRICTED AND COMMUNAL KNOWLEDGE

Because of the truth-value accorded to the images, shaman/artists could manipulate design elements and graphic representations of hallucinatory experiences in response to variable environmental challenges or to suit specific political purposes. Power struggles between shamans are not only reflected in but also negotiated through rock art imagery (Dowson 1998). The lower Pecos rock art may have served to negotiate power struggles, whether metaphysical or historical in origin (see chap. 5). The tension illustrated in art and myth between peyote and datura, and their animal counterparts, deer and coyote, may reflect a struggle for power between two historical shamans. If not historical in origin, it reflects a struggle for power at the metaphysical level. It is important to remember that for shamans, supernatural relations are as real as the everyday "natural" social relations. "The images of spirits . . . are in a sense like people in prehistory. They are as much people as the shamans who experienced them and the artists who painted them" (Dowson 1998:341).

Rock Art and Ideology

Artists of the lower Pecos communicated the structure of their cosmos and messages from the supernatural realm to their community through art. The information communicated through the art can be used today to reconstruct aspects of lower Pecos cosmos and to identify specific rituals performed during the Archaic period.

A TIERED UNIVERSE

The journey motif graphically illustrates belief in a tiered cosmos with a supernatural realm residing beyond the serpent—a metaphor for the earth's surface. Passage to the otherworld was possible through features in the natural landscape, such as caves, sinkholes, and other openings in the earth's surface. Entering the mouth of a cave or sinkhole was symbolic of entering the mouth of the serpent or passing through the body of a serpent to access the supernatural realm. The lower Pecos practice of burying the dead in sinkholes and horizontal shaft caves was a means of returning the dead to the land of the ancestors.

THE PEYOTE SACRAMENT

Accessing the supernatural realm was also facilitated through the consumption of the peyote sacrament. Identification of peyotism in pictographs of the lower Pecos has important contributions to make, not only to the reconstruction of hunting and gathering lifeways in the lower Pecos but also to the debate regarding origins of the peyote religion. Generally recognized as having its origins in northern Mexico and southern Texas along the Rio

Grande, the earliest historical reference to peyotism appears in accounts of hunter-gatherer *mitote* ceremonies conducted during the 1500s. The identification of peyotism in the lower Pecos rock art potentially extends the origins of peyotism back at least four thousand years.

Motif B, which has been identified at several sites in the region, demonstrates that a metaphorical relationship existed in the lower Pecos Archaic period between deer and peyote. Further analysis of the rock art panel at the White Shaman site (41VV124) resulted in the identification of specific details in lower Pecos peyotism. Although peyote had been previously identified in Archaic period archaeological deposits, prior to the incorporation of pictographic data, the importance of this plant was not known. The prevalence of this motif in lower Pecos rock art and the identification of peyote in the archaeological sediments, suggests that peyote was an important medicinal and sacramental plant used by the hunter-gatherers of the lower Pecos River region during the Archaic period.

DATURA AND SHAMANISM

Motif C reflects the pictographic representation of *Datura* spp. *Datura* spp., an important plant used as medicine and as a bridge to the otherworld, was also identified in lower Pecos Archaic period archaeological deposits. Datura has been an important medicinal and hallucinogenic plant in both the Old and New World. In the ethnographic literature, datura use by shamans for the purpose of divination, curing, prophecy, ecstatic initiation, and ritual intoxication is widely reported. The datura motif appears in the Pecos River–style rock art throughout the region, suggesting its importance in lower Pecos hunter-gatherer pharmacopeia.

In the preceding pages, I have begun to unveil the work of art in the lower Pecos and, I hope, contributed to our understanding of the Archaic hunter-gatherers of the region. The production of rock art was an integral part of lower Pecos hunter-gatherer adaptation: it communicated information regarding the bio-physical environment of the region, animal behavior, and ecological relationships important for the successful exploitation of the hunting and gathering niche. Both the art and the artist were active agents in creating, maintaining, and transforming social relations and religious identities. The art was a vehicle through which individual intangible assets were shared—individual knowledge became group knowledge. The rock art was ingrained in the technological, social, and ideological business of the hunting and gathering community within which it was produced; the art performed work. Production of art was an adaptive response to challenges in the social and physical environment.

Prehistoric art is not beyond explanation. Images from the past contain a vast corpus of data—accessible through proven, scientific methods—that can enrich our understanding of human lifeways in prehistory and, at the same time, expand our appreciation for the work of art in the present and the future.

Appendix

REPORTING FORMS
FOR ROCK ART

SITE FORM

Site no.: _____ Recorder(s) _____

Date: _____ Location: UTM zone _____ USGS map name: _____

Time of day: _____ Best lighting: _____ Easting ___ ___ ___ ___ ___ ___ ___

Northing ___ ___ ___ ___ ___ ___ ___

Previously recorded: yes   no   If yes, by: _____

If yes, location of documentation: _____

_____

Site owner (name, address, phone no.): _____

_____

Description of site location: _____

_____

Directions for site access: _____

_____

Type of site: shelter _____ cliff face _____ other _____

Habitation site: _____ Mortar holes: _____

Rock art category: pictograph _____ petroglyph _____ both _____

Exposure (direction rock art faces): _____ Dimensions of decorated area: _____

Present condition of site: _____

_____

_____

Brief description/Present condition of rock art: _____

_____

_____

_____

Natural deterioration: _____

_____

Vandalism: _____

_____

Nearest natural water source (include approx. distance): _____

_____

Vegetation: _____

_____

_____

PHOTO REFERENCE FORM

Photo reference no.: _____   Roll no.: _____

Photographers: _____   Film type: _____

Site no.: _____   Date: _____

	SUBJECT	UNIT NO.	TIME	F/EXP	LENS	FILTER	COMMENTS
1.							
2.							
3.							
4.							
5.							
6.							
7.							
8.							
9.							
10.							
11.							
12.							
13.							
14.							
15.							
16.							
17.							
18.							
19.							
20.							
21.							
22.							
23.							
24.							
25.							
26							
27.							
28.							
29.							
30.							
31.							
32.							
33.							
34.							
35.							
36.							

ZOOMORPHS FORM

Site no.: _____   Recorder(s): _____

Photo reference no.: _____   Date: _____

Deer _____	
Canines _____	
Felines _____	
Birds _____	
Reptiles _____	

CENTRASTYLED (SKELETONIZED) ANTHROPOMORPHS FORM

Site no.: _____

Recorder(s): _____

Photo reference no.: _____

Date: _____

CENTRASTYLED ANTHROPOMORPHS (NONTHERIANTHROPIC)

Page ____ of ____

NONCENTRASTYLED (NONSKELETONIZED) ANTHROPOMORPHS FORM

Site no.: _____

Recorder(s): _____

Photo reference no.: _____

Date: _____

NONCENTRASTYLED ANTHROPOMORPHS

THERIANTHROPES FORM

Site no.: _____   Recorder(s): _____

Photo reference no.: _____   Date: _____

THERIANTHROPES   Page _____ of _____

HANDPRINTS AND GEOMETRICS FORM

Site no.: _____   Recorder(s): _____

Photo reference no.: _____   Date: _____

HANDPRINTS (NEGATIVE   POSITIVE   STYLIZED   )   Page ____ of ____

GEOMETRICS

SUBJECT FORM

Site no.: _____   Recorder(s): _____

Photo reference no.: _____   Date: _____

SUBJECT: _____   Page ____ of ____

Bibliography

Aberle, D. F. 1966. *The Peyote Religion among the Navajo.* Chicago: Aldine.

Adovasio, J. M., and G. F. Fry. 1976. Prehistoric Psychotropic Drug Use in Northeastern Mexico and Trans-Pecos Texas. *Economic Botany* 30:94–96.

Amos, B., and F. Gehlbach, eds. 1988. *Edwards Plateau Vegetation: Plant Ecological Studies in Texas.* Waco, Tex.: Baylor University Press.

Anderson, E. F. 1996. *Peyote: The Divine Cactus.* 2nd ed. Tucson: University of Arizona Press.

Anderson, R. L. 1979. *Art in Primitive Societies.* Englewood Cliffs, N.J.: Prentice-Hall.

———. 1990. *Calliope's Sisters: A Comparative Study of Philosophies of Art.* Englewood Cliffs, N.J.: Prentice Hall.

———. 2000. *American Muse: Anthropological Excursions into Art and Aesthetics.* Upper Saddle River, N.J.: Prentice Hall

Andrews, R. L., and J. M. Adovasio. 1980. *Perishable Industries from Hinds Cave, Val Verde County, Texas.* Ethnology Monographs 5. Pittsburgh: University of Pittsburgh.

Applegate, R. B. 1975. The Datura Cult among the Chumash. *Journal of California Anthropology* 2:7–17.

Archer, S. 1990. Development and Stability of Grass/Woody Mosaics in a Subtropical Savanna Parkland, Texas, U.S.A. *Journal of Biogeography* 17:453–62.

———. 1995. Tree-grass Dynamics in a *Prosopis*-Thornscrub Savannah Parkland: Reconstructing the Past and Predicting the Future. *Ecoscience* 2(1):84–99.

Archer, S., C. Scifres, C. Bassham, and R. Maggio. 1988. Autogenic Succession in a Subtropical Savannah: Conversion of Grassland to Thorn Woodland. *Ecological Monographs* 58(2):111–27.

Aveleyra, L., M. Maldonado, and P. Martinez. 1956. *Cueva de la Candelaria.* Mexico: Memorias del Instituto Nacional de Antropologia e Historia V.

Avery, A. G., S. Satina, and J. Rietsema. 1959. *Blakeslee: The Genus Datura.* New York: Ronald Press.

Bahr, D. M. 1974. *Pima Shamanism and Staying Sickness (Ká:cim Mumkidag).* Tucson: University of Arizona Press.

Barasch, M. 1998. *Modern Theories of Art, 2: From Impressionism to Kadinsky.* New York: New York University Press.

Barber, E. W. 1994. *Women's Work: The First 20,000 Years.* New York: Norton.

Barrows, D. P. 1900. *The Ethno-botany of the Coahuilla Indians of Southern California.* University of Chicago Press, Chicago.

Bass, P. 1989. The Pecos Project: Semiotic Models for the Study of Rock Art. Ph.D. diss., Rice University, Houston.

———. 1994. A Gendered Search through Some West Texas Rock Art. In *New Light on Old Art: Recent Research Advances in Hunter-Gatherer Rock Art Research,* edited by D. S. Whitley and L. L. Loendorf. Monograph 36. Los Angeles: Institute of Archaeology, University of California.

Bassie-Sweet, K. 1991. *From the Mouth of the Dark Cave.* Norman: University of Oklahoma Press.

Beals, R. L. 1943. *The Aboriginal Cultures of the Cahita Indians.* Ibero-Americana No. 19. Berkeley: University of California.

———. 1973. *The Comparative Ethnology of Northern Mexico before 1750.* Ibero-Americana No. 2. 1932. Reprint, New York: Cooper Square.

Bean, L. J., and K. S. Saubel. 1972. *Temalpakh (from the Earth): Cahuilla Indian Knowledge and Usage of Plants.* Morongo Indian Reservation: Malki Museum Press.

Bement, L. C. 1989. Lower Pecos Canyonlands. In *From the Gulf to the Rio Grande: Human Adaptation in Central, South, and Lower Pecos Texas,* edited by T. R. Hester, pp. 63–76. Research Series 33. Fayetteville: Arkansas Archaeological Survey.

—————. 1994. *Hunter-Gatherer Mortuary Practices during the Central Texas Archaic.* Texas Archaeology and Ethnohistory Series. Austin: University of Texas Press.

Benitez, F. 1975. *In the Magic Land of Peyote.* Austin: University of Texas Press.

Bennet, W. C., and R. M. Zingg. 1935. *The Tarahumara: An Indian Tribe of Northern Mexico.* Chicago: University of Chicago Press.

Berrin, K., ed. 1978. *Art of the Huichol Indians.* New York: Harry Abrams.

Bettinger, R. L., R. Boyd, and P. Richerson. 1996. Style, Function, and Cultural Evolutionary Process. In *Darwinian Archaeologies,* edited by H. D. Graham and G. Maschner, pp. 133–64. New York: Plenum Press.

Biesele, M. 1976. Aspects of !Kung Folklore. In *Kalahari Hunter-Gatherers,* edited by R. B. Lee and I. DeVore, pp. 302–24. Cambridge: Harvard University Press.

—————. 1983. Interpretation in Rock Art and Folklore: Communication Systems in Evolutionary Perspective. In *New Approaches to Southern African Rock Art,* edited by J. D. Lewis-Williams, pp. 54–60. Goodwin Series. Vol. 4. Cape Town: South African Archaeological Society.

Black, S. L. 1986. *The Clement and Hermina Hinojosa Site 41JW8: A Toyah Horizon Campsite in Southern Texas.* Special Report No. 18. San Antonio: Center for Archaeological Research, University of Texas.

Blackburn, T. 1975. *December's Child: A Book of Chumash Oral Narratives.* Berkeley: University of California Press.

—————. 1977. Biophysical Aspects of Chumash Rock Art. *Journal of California Anthropology* 4(1):88–94.

Blair, W. F. 1950. The Biotic Provinces of Texas. *Texas Journal of Science* 2:93–117.

Blurton Jones, N., and M. Konner. 1976. !Kung Knowledge of Animal Behaviour, or: The Proper Study of Mankind Is Animals. In *Kalahari Hunter-Gatherers,* edited by R. B. Lee and I. DeVore, pp. 325–48. Cambridge: Harvard University Press.

Boke, N. H., and E. F. Anderson. 1970. Structure, Development, and Taxonomy in the Genus Lophophora. *American Journal of Botany* 57(5):569–78.

Boone, J. L., and E. A. Smith. 1998. Is It Evolution Yet?: A Critique of Evolutionary Archaeology. *Current Anthropology* 39(3):141–73.

Boyd, C. E. 1993. Rediscovering the Paint of the Pecos River Style Pictographs. Paper presented at the 64th Annual Meeting of the Texas Archaeological Society, Laredo, Tex.

—————. 1996. Shamanic Journeys into the Otherworld of the Archaic Chichimec. *Latin American Antiquity* 7(2):152–64.

—————. 1998. Pictographic Evidence of Peyotism in the Lower Pecos, Texas, Archaic. In *The Archaeology of Rock Art,* edited by C. Chippindale and P. S. C. Taçon. Cambridge: Cambridge University Press.

Boyd, C. E., and J. P. Dering. 1996. Medicinal and Hallucinogenic Plants Identified in the Sediments and the Pictographs of the Lower Pecos, Texas, Archaic. *Antiquity* 70(268):256–75.

Brown, D. E. 1982. Chihuahuan Desertscrub. *Desert Plants* 4:169–79.

Brown, K. 1991. Prehistoric Economics at Baker Cave: A Plan for Research. In *Papers on Lower Pecos Prehistory,* edited by S. A. Turpin, pp. 87–140. Studies in Archaeology 8. Austin: Texas Archaeological Research Laboratory, University of Texas.

Bruhn, J. G., and B. Holmstedt. 1974. Early Peyote Research: An Interdisciplinary Study. *Economic Botany* 28:353–90.

Brundage, B. C. 1979. *The Fifth Sun: Aztec Gods, Aztec World.* Austin: University of Texas Press.

Bryant, V. M., Jr. 1969. Late Full-Glacial and Post-glacial Pollen Analysis of Texas Sediments. Ph.D. diss., University of Texas.

—————. 1974. Prehistoric Diet in Southwest Texas. *American Antiquity* 39:407–20.

Bryant, V. M., Jr., and R. G. Holloway. 1985. A Late Quaternary Paleoenvironmental Record of Texas: An Overview of the Pollen Evidence. In *Pollen Records of the Late Quaternary North American Sediments,* edited by V. M. Bryant, Jr., and R. G. Holloway, pp. 39–70. Dallas: American Association of Stratigraphic Palynologists Foundation.

Bye, R. 1979. Hallucinogenic Plants of the Tarahumara. *Journal of Ethnopharmacology* 1:23–48.

—————. 1985. Medicinal Plants of the Tarahumara Indians of Chihuahua, Mexico. In *Two Mummies from Chihuahua Mexico,* edited by R. Tyson and D. Elerick, pp. 77–104. San Diego Museum Papers 19, San Diego.

Bye, R., R. Mata, and J. Pimentel. 1991. Botany, Ethnobotany, and Chemistry of *Datura Lanosa* (Solanacae) in Mexico. *Anales del Insituto Biológica, Universidad Nacional Autónomo, Serie Botánica* 61(1):21–42.

Campbell, T. N. 1947. The Fields Shelter: An Archaeological Site in Edwards County, Texas. *Texas Journal of Science* 9:7–25.

—————. 1958. Origin of the Mescal Bean Cult. *American Anthropologist* 60(1):156–60.

—————. 1988. The Indians of Southeastern Texas and Northeastern Mexico: Selected Writings of Thomas Nolan Campbell. Texas Archaeological Research Laboratory, Balcones Research Center, University of Texas.

Chaffee, S. D., M. Hyman, and M. Rowe. 1993. AMS C14 Dating of Rock Paintings. In *Time and Space,* edited by J. Steinbring, A. Watchman, P. Faulstich, and P. S. C. Taçon. Australian Rock Art Research Association, Occasional AURA Publication 8, Melbourne.

—————. 1994. Radiocarbon Dating of Rock Paintings. In *New Light on Old Art: Recent Advances in Hunter-Gatherer Rock Art Research,* edited by D. S. Whitley and L. L. Loendorf. Monograph 36. Los Angeles: Institute of Archaeology, University of California.

Clottes, J. 1989. The Identification of Human and Animal Figures in European Paleolithic Art. In *Animals into Art,* edited by H. Morphy, pp. 21–56. Vol. 7. London: Unwin Hyman.

Conkey, M. 1984. To Find Ourselves: Art and Social Geography of Prehistoric Hunter Gatherers. In *Past and Present in Hunter Gatherer Studies,* edited by C. Schrire, pp. 253–76. Orlando: Academic Press.

Cooke, B., and F. Turner, eds. 1999. *Biopoetics: Evolutionary Explorations in the Arts.* Lexington, Ky.: ICUS.

Cooke, J. L. 1993. Assessing Populations in Complex Systems. Ph.D. diss., Texas A&M University, College Station.

Cooper, S. 1971. A Dissertation on the Properties and Effects of the Common Thorn-Apple and Its Uses in Medicine. Ph.D. diss., University of Pittsburgh.

Cotter, H. 1997. Beyond Beauty: Art That Takes Action. *New York Times,* September 28, 1997, p. 35.

Cutler, H. C. 1956. The Plant Remains. In *Higgins Flat Pueblo: Western New Mexico,* edited by P. S. Martin, J. B. Rinaldo, E. A. Bluhm, and H. C. Cutler, pp. 174–83. Fieldiana, Anthropology. Vol. 45. Chicago: Chicago National History Museum.

Cutler, H. C., and L. Kaplan. 1956. Some Plant Remains from Montezuma Castle and Nearby Caves (NA 4007B and C and on Dry Beaver Creek). *Plateau* 28:98–100.

Davenport, J. W. 1938. *Archaeological Exploration of Eagle Cave.* Big Bend Basket Maker Papers 4. San Antonio: Witte Museum.

Dering, J. P. 1979. Pollen and Plant Macrofossil Vegetation Record Recovered from Hinds Cave, Val Verde County, Texas. Master's thesis, Texas A&M University, College Station.

—————. 1998. *Archaeological Context and Land Use in the Western Rio Grande Plains.* Technical Report 1. College Station: Center for Ecological Archaeology, Texas A&M University.

—————. 1999. Earth Oven Plant Processing in Archaic Period Economies: An Example from a Semi-Arid Savannah in South-Central North America. *American Antiquity* 64(4): 659–74.

Dibble, D. S. 1967. *Excavation of Arenosa Shelter.* University of Texas. Report Submitted to the National Park Service by the Texas Archaeological Salvage Project.

Dibble, D. S., and D. Lorrain. 1968. *Bonfire Shelter: A Stratified Bison Kill Site, Val Verde County, Texas.* Miscellaneous Papers. Austin: Texas Memorial Museum, University of Texas.

Dissanayake, E. 1988. *What Is Art For?* Seattle: University of Washington Press.

—————. 1992. *Homo Aestheticus: Where Art Comes From and Why.* New York: Free Press.

Ditton R. B., and D. J. Schmidly. 1977. *A User Resource Analysis of Amistad Recreation Area.* Prepared for the Office of Natural Resources, Southwest Region, National Park Service, Santa Fe, New Mexico. Contract No cx702960169. Texas Agricultural Experiment Station, Texas A&M University, College Station.

Dobkin de Rios, M. 1973. Curing with Ayahuasca in an Urban Slum. In *Hallucinogens and Shamanism,* edited by M. J. Harner, pp. 67–85. New York: Oxford University Press.

—————. 1984. *Hallucinogens: Cross-Cultural Perspectives.* Albuquerque: University of New Mexico Press.

Dobkin de Rios, M., and M. Winkleman. 1989. Shamanism and Altered States of Consciousness. *Journal of Psychoactive Drugs* 21(1):1–7.

Dowson, T. A. 1988. Revelations of Religious Reality: The Individual in San Art. *World Archaeology* 20:116–28.

—————. 1994. Reading Art, Writing History: Rock Art and Social Change in Southern Africa. *World Archaeology* 25(3):332–45.

—————. 1998. Like People in Prehistory. *World Archaeology* 28(3):333–43.

Driver, H. 1969. *Indians of North America.* Chicago: University of Chicago Press.

Dupre, W. 1975. *Religion in Primitive Cultures: A Study in Ethnophilosophy.* The Hague: Mouton.

Eastwood, R. 1893. General Notes of a Trip through Southwestern Utah. *Zoe* 3:354–61.

Eliade, M. 1959. *The Sacred and the Profane.* New York: Harcourt Brace Jovanovich.

—————. 1964. *Shamanism: Archaic Techniques of Ecstacy.* Princeton, N.J.: Princeton University Press.

Eliot, J. 1998. Hunting Prowess from Plants. *National Geographic* 4:142.

Elmore, F. H. 1943. *Ethnobotany of the Navajo.* University of Mexico Bulletin. Monograph Series 1(7). Albuquerque: University of New Mexico Press.

Epstein, J. 1969. *The San Isidro Site: An Early Man Campsite in Nuevo Leon, Mexico.* Anthropological Series No. 7. Austin: Department of Anthropology, University of Texas.

Evans, W. 1979. Tropane Alkaloids of the Solanaceae. In *Biology and Taxonomy of the Solanaceae,* edited by J. Hawkes, R. Lester, and A. Skelding, pp. 241–54. London: Academic Press.

Fackelmann, K. A. 1993. Food, Drug, or Poison?: Cultivating a Taste for Toxic Plants. *Science News* 143:312–15.

Favata, M. A., and J. B. Fernandez. 1993. *The Account: Álvar Núñez Cabeza de Vaca's Relación.* Houston: Arte Público Press.

Fenneman, N. M. 1931. *Physiography of Western United States.* New York: McGraw-Hill.

Forge, J. A. 1967. The Abelam Artist. In *Social Organization: Essays Presented to Raymond Firth,* edited by M. Freedman, pp. 65–84. London: Cass.

Furst, P. T. 1972. *Flesh of the Gods.* New York: Praeger.

———. 1976. *Hallucinogens and Culture.* Novato, Calif.: Chandler and Sharp.

———. 1978. The Art of Being Huichol. In *Art of the Huichol Indians,* edited by K. Berrin, pp. 18–34. New York: Harry Abrams.

———. 1989. Review of *Peyote Religion: A History. American Ethnologist* 16(2):386–87.

Furst, P. T., and B. G. Myerhoff. 1966. Myth as History: The Jimsonweed Cycle of the Huichols of Mexico. *Anthropologica* 17:3–39.

Gebhard, D. 1965. *Prehistoric Paintings of the Seminole Canyon Area, Val Verde County, Texas.* Report Submitted to the National Park Service, Southwest Region.

Golden, M. L., W. J. Gabriel, and J. W. Stevens. 1982. *Soil Survey of Val Verde County, Texas.* Washington, D.C.: U.S. Department of Agriculture, Soil Conservation Service.

Goodman, F. D., J. Henney, and E. Pressel. 1974. *Trance, Healing, and Hallucination.* New York: John Wiley and Sons.

Grieder, T. 1966. Periods in Pecos River Style Pictographs. *American Antiquity* 31:710–20.

Griffen, W. B. 1969. *Culture Change and Shifting Population in Central Northern Mexico.* Anthropological Papers No. 13. Tucson: University of Arizona Press.

Harner, M. J. 1973a. *Hallucinogens and Shamanism.* New York: Oxford University Press.

———. 1973b. Hallucinogens in European Witchcraft. In *Hallucinogens and Shamanism,* edited by M. J. Harner, pp. 125–50. New York: Oxford University Press.

Hatch, S. L., K. N. Gandhi, and L. E. Brown. 1990. *Checklist of the Vascular Plants of Texas.* Publication MP-1655. College Station: Texas Agricultural Experiment Station, Texas A&M University.

Hatfield, G. M., J. J. Valdes, W. L. Merrill, and V. H. Jones. 1977. An Investigation of the *Sophora Secundiflora* Seeds (Mescal Beans). *LLoydia* 40(4):374–83.

Hedges, K. 1976. Southern California Rock Art as Shamanic Art. In *American Indian Rock Art* 2:126–38.

———. 1982. Phosphenes in the Context of Native American Rock Art. *American Indian Rock Art* 5: 51–58.

———. 1994. Pipette Dreams and the Primordial Snake-Canoe: Analysis of a Hallucinatory Form Constant. In *Shamanism and Rock Art in North America,* edited by S. Turpin, pp 103–24. San Antonio: Rock Art Foundation.

———. 1994. Shamanic Origins of Rock Art. In *Ancient Images on Stone,* edited by J. A. Von Tilberg, pp. 46–61. Los Angeles: UCLS Institute of Archaeology, Rock Art Archive.

Heiser, T. R. 1989. *Nightshades: The Paradoxical Plants.* San Francisco: W. H. Freeman.

Hesse, E. 1946. *Narcotics and Drug Addiction.* New York: Philosophical Library.

Hester, T. 1980. *Digging into South Texas Prehistory.* San Antonio: Corona.

———. 1983. Late Paleo-Indian Occupations at Baker Cave, Southwestern Texas. *Bulletin of the Texas Archeological Society* 53:101–19.

———. 1995. The Prehistory of South Texas. *Bulletin of the Texas Archeological Society* 66:427–60.

Hester, T. R., H. J. Shafer, and K. L. Feder. 1997. *Field Methods in Archaeology.* 7th ed. Mountain View, Calif.: Mayfield.

Heyden, D. 1981. Caves, Gods, and Myths: World-View and Planning of Teotihuacan. In *Mesoamerican Sites and World-Views,* edited by E. Benson, pp. 1–37. Washington, D.C.: Dunbarton Oaks.

Holden, W. C. 1937. Excavation of Murrah Cave. *Texas Archaeological and Paleontological Society* 9:48–73.

Horowitz, M. J. 1964. The Imagery of Visual Hallucinations. *Journal of Nervous and Mental Disease* 138:513–23.

———. 1975. Hallucinations: An Information-Processing Approach. In *Hallucinations: Behavior, Experience, and Theory,* edited by R. K. Siegel and L. J. West, pp. 163–95. New York: Wiley.

Howard, J. H. 1957. The Mescal Bean Cult of the Central and Southern Plains: An Ancestor of the Peyote Cult? *American Anthropologist* 59:75–87.

———. 1960. Mescalism and Peyotism Once Again. *Plains Anthropologist* 5:84–85.

Hoyt, C. A. 2000. Grassland to Desert: Holocene Vegetation and Climatic Change in the Northern Chihuahuan Desert. Ph.D. dissertation, University of Texas, Austin.

Hrdlicka, A. 1908. *Physical and Medical Observations among the Indians of Southwestern United States and Northern Mexico.* Bureau of American Ethnology. Bulletin 34. Smithsonian Institution. Washington, D.C.: Government Printing Office.

Hultkrantz, Å. 1968. The Ecological and Phenomenological Aspects of Shamanism. In *Shamanism in Siberia,* edited by B. Dioszegi and M. Hoppal. Budapest: Akademiai Kiado.

———. 1997. *The Attraction of Peyote: An Inquiry into the Basic Conditions for the Diffusion of the Peyote Religion of North America.* Stockholm: Almqvist and Wiksell International.

Hyman, M., and M. W. Rowe. 1997. Plasma-Chemical

Extraction and AMS Radiocarbon Dating of Pictographs. *American Indian Rock Art* 23:1–9.

Ilger, W. A., M. Hyman, and M. W. Rowe. 1994.
Radiocarbon Date for a Red Linear Style Pictograph.
Bulletin of the Texas Archaeological Society 65:337–46.

Ilger, W. A., M. Hyman, J. Southon, and M. W. Rowe.
1995. Dating Pictographs with Radiocarbon. *Radiocarbon* 37(2):299–310.

Ireland, W. M. 1817. *Remarks on the Medical Properties of
the Stramonium: Being Series of Facts and Observations
Made for the Purpose of Ascertaining the Qualities and
Effects of that Valuable Plant.* New York.

Irwin, L. 1994. *The Dream Seekers: Native American
Visionary Traditions of the Great Plains.* Norman: University of Oklahoma Press.

Jackson, A. T. 1938. *Picture-Writing of Texas Indians.*
Austin: University of Texas.

Johnson, L., Jr. 1994. *The Life and Times of Toyah-Culture
Folk: The Buckhollow Encampment, Site 41KM16, Kimble
County, Texas.* Office of the State Archaeologist,
Report 38. Texas Department of Transportation
and Texas Historical Commission, Austin.

Kalweit, H. 1988. *Dreamtime and Inner Space: The World
of the Shaman.* Translated by Werner Wünsche.
Boston: Shambhala.

Katz, R., M. Biesele, and V. St. Denis. 1997. *Healing
Makes Our Hearts Happy: Spirituality and Cultural
Transformation among the Kalahari Ju/'hoansi.*
Rochester, Vt.: Inner Traditions.

Kelley, J. C. 1950. Atlatls, Bows and Arrows, Pictographs, and the Pecos River Focus. *American Antiquity*
16(1):71–74.

———. 1971. Pictorial and Ceramic Art in Mexican
Cultural Littoral of the Chichimec Sea. In *Art and
Environment in Native America,* edited by M. E. King
and I. R. Traylor, pp. 23–54. Special Publication of
the Museum. Lubbock: Texas Tech University.

———. 1974. Speculations on the Culture History
of Northwestern Mesoamerica. In *The Archaeology
of West Mexico,* edited by B. Bell, pp. 19–39.
Ajijic, Mexico: West Mexican Society for Advanced Study.

Kelly, R. L. 1995. *The Foraging Spectrum: Diversity in
Hunter-Gatherer Lifeways.* Washington, D.C.: Smithsonian Institution Press.

Kirch, P. 1980. The Archaeological Study of Adaptation: Theoretical and Methodological Issues. In
Advances in Archaeological Method and Theory, edited
by M. B. Schiffer, pp. 101–56. Vol. 3. London:
Academic Press.

Kirkland, F. 1938. A Description of Texas Pictographs.
*Bulletin of the Texas Archaeological and Paleontological
Society* 1:11–40.

Kirkland, F., and W. W. Newcomb. 1967. *The Rock Art
of Texas Indians.* Austin: University of Texas Press.

Klein-Schwartz, W., and G. Oderda. 1984. Jimsonweed Intoxication in Adolescents and Young Adults.
American Journal of Disease in Children 138:737–39.

Kluckhohn, C. 1944. *Navaho Witchcraft.* Boston: Beacon
Press.

Klüver, H. 1926. Mescal Visions and Eidetic Vision.
American Journal of Psychology 37:502–15.

———. 1942. Mechanisms of Hallucinations. In
Studies in Personality, edited by Q. McNemar and
M. A. Merrill, pp. 175–207. New York:
McGraw-Hill.

———. 1966. *Mescal and the Mechanisms of Hallucinations.* Chicago: University of Chicago Press.

Knab, T. 1977. Notes Concerning Use of *Solandra*
among the Huichol. *Economic Botany* 31:80–86.

Krippner, S. 1985. *Learning Guide for the Psychology of
Shamanism.* San Francisco: Saybrook Institute.

Kristeller, P. O. 1970. The Modern System of the Arts.
In *Problems in Aesthetics,* edited by M. Weitz,
pp. 108–64. 2nd ed. New York: Macmillan.

Kulig, K., and B. Rumack. 1983. Anticholinergic
Poisoning. In *Clinical Management of Poisoning and
Drug Overdose,* edited by L. Haddad and J. Win-
chester, pp. 482–87. Philadelphia: W. B. Saunders.

La Barre, W. 1957. Mescalism and Peyotism. *American
Anthropologist* 59:708–11.

———. 1975. *The Peyote Cult.* 4th ed. New York:
Schocken Books.

Layton, R. 1992. *Australian Rock Art: A New Synthesis.*
Cambridge: Cambridge University Press.

Lemaistre, D. 1996. The Deer that is Peyote and the
Deer that is Maiz. In *People of the Peyote: Huichol
Indian History, Religion, and Survival,* edited by
S. Schaefer and P. Furst, pp. 308–29. Albuquerque:
University of New Mexico Press.

Leroi-Gourhan, A. 1982. *The Dawn of European Art: An
Introduction to Paleolithic Cave Painting.* Cambridge:
Cambridge University Press.

———. 1993. *Gesture and Speech.* Cambridge: MIT
Press.

Lewis, W. H., and M. P. F. Elvin-Lewis. 1977. *Medical
Botany: Plants Affecting Man's Health.* New York: John
Wiley and Sons.

Lewis-Williams, J. D. 1980. Ethnography and Iconography: Aspects of Southern San Thought and Art.
Man 15:467–82.

———. 1981. *Believing and Seeing : Symbolic Meanings
in Southern African Rock Painting.* London: Academic
Press.

———. 1982. The Economic and Social Context of
Southern San Rock Art. *Current Anthropology*
23:429–49.

———. 1983. Introductory Essay: Science and Rock
Art. In *New Approaches to Southern African Rock Art,*
edited by J. D. Lewis-Williams, pp. 3–13. Goodwin
Series. No. 4. Cape Town: South African Archaeological Society.

———. 1984a. The Empiricist Impasse in Southern African Rock Art Studies. *South African Archaeological Bulletin* 39:58–66.

———. 1984b. Ideological Continuities in Prehistoric Southern Africa: The Evidence of Rock Art. In *Past and Present in Hunter Gatherer Studies,* edited by C. Schrire. Orlando: Academic Press.

———. 1986a. Cognitive and Optical Illusions in San Rock Art Research. *Current Anthropology* 27:171–78.

———. 1986b. The Last Testament of the Southern San. *South African Archaeological Bulletin* 41:10–11.

———. 1987. A Dream of Eland: An Unexplored Component of San Shamanism and Rock Art. *World Archaeology* 19:165–77.

———. 1989. Southern Africa's Place in the Archaeology of Human Understanding. *South African Journal of Science* 85:45–52.

———. 1990. Documentation, Analysis, and Interpretation: Problems in Rock Art Research. *South African Archaeological Bulletin* 45:126–36.

———. 1992. Ethnographic Evidence Relating to "Trance" and "Shamans" among Northern and Southern Bushmen. *South African Archaeological Bulletin* 47:56–60.

———. 1993. Southern African Archaeology in the 1990s. *South African Archaeological Bulletin* 48:45–50.

———. 1995a. Modeling the Production and Consumption of Rock Art. *South African Archaeological Bulletin* 50:143–54.

———. 1995b. Seeing and Construing: The Making and "Meaning" of a Southern African Rock Art Motif. *Cambridge Archaeological Journal* 5(1):3–23.

Lewis-Williams, J. D., and M. Biesele. 1978. Eland Hunting Rituals among Northern and Southern San Groups: Striking Similarities. *Africa* 48:117–34.

Lewis-Williams, J. D., and T. A. Dowson. 1988. Signs of All Times: Entoptic Phenomena in Upper Paleolithic Art. *Current Anthropology* 29:201–45.

———. 1989. *Images of Power: Understanding Bushman Rock Art.* Johannesburg: Southern Book.

———. 1990. Through the Veil: San Rock Paintings and the Rock Face. *South African Archaeological Bulletin* 45:5–16.

Lewis-Williams, J. D., T. A. Dowson, and J. Deacon. 1993. Rock Art and Changing Perceptions of Southern Africa's Past: Ezeljagdspoort Reviewed. *Antiquity* 67:273–91.

Litovitz, T. 1983. Hallucinogens. In *Clinical Management of Poisoning and Drug Overdose,* edited by L. Haddad and J. Winchester, pp. 455–82. Philadelphia: W. B. Saunders.

Lord, K. J. 1984. The Zooarchaeology of Hinds Cave (41vv456). Ph.D. diss., University of Texas, Austin.

Lumholtz, C. 1900. *Symbolism of the Huichol Indians.* Memoirs. Vol. 3. New York: American Museum of Natural History.

———. 1902. *Unknown Mexico.* Vol. 2. New York: Scribner's.

———. 1903. Explorations in Mexico. *Geographical Journal* 21:126–42.

Maclay, W., and E. Guttman. 1941. Mescaline Hallucinations in Artists. *Archives of Neurology and Psychiatry* 45:130–38.

Mahler, D. A. 1975. The Jimsonweed High. *Journal of the American Medical Association* 231(2):138.

Manhire, A., J. Parkington, and W. van Rijssen. 1983. A Distributional Approach to the Interpretation of Rock Art in the South-western Cape. In *New Approaches to Southern African Rock Art,* edited by J. D. Lewis-Williams. Goodwin Series. Vol. 4. Cape Town: South African Archaeological Society.

Maquet, J. 1971. *Introduction to Aesthetic Anthropology.* Reading, Mass.: Addison-Wesley.

———. 1986. *The Aesthetic Experience: An Anthropologist Looks at the Visual Arts.* New Haven: Yale University Press.

Marks, M. K., J. C. Rose, and E. L. Buie. 1985. Bioarchaeology of Seminole Sink. In *Excavation of a Vertical Shaft Tomb, Val Verde County, Texas,* edited by S. Turpin, pp. 75–118. Austin: University of Texas.

Marmaduke, W. S. 1978. Prehistoric Culture in Trans-Pecos Texas: An Ecological Approach. Ph.D. diss., University of Texas, Austin.

Martin, G. C. 1933. *Archaeological Exploration of the Shumla Caves.* Witte Museum Memorial Bulletin 3. San Antonio: Witte Memorial Museum.

Martinez, M. 1969. *Las Plantas Medicinales de México.* 5th ed. Mexico: Ediciones Botas.

Mawk, E. 1999. Reexamination of Ancient DNA in Texas Rock Paintings. Ph.D. diss., Texas A&M University, College Station.

McGregor, R. 1992. *Prehistoric Basketry of the Lower Pecos, Texas.* Monographs in World Archaeology 6. Madison: Prehistory Press.

Merrill, W. L. 1977. *An Investigation of the Ethnographic and Archaeological Specimens of Mescal Beans* (Sophora Secundiflora) *in American Museums.* Research Reports in Ethnobotany, Technical Report 6. Ann Arbor: University of Michigan.

Millspaugh, C. F. 1974. *American Medicinal Plants.* New York: Dover.

Moises, R., J. Holden Kelly, and W. C. Holden. 1971. *A Yaqui Life: The Personal Chronicle of a Yaqui Indian.* Lincoln: University of Nebraska Press.

Morgan, G. R. 1983. The Biogeography of Peyote in South Texas. In *Botanical Museum Leaflets,* pp. 73–86. Vol. 29. Cambridge: Harvard University.

Morphy, H. 1991. *Ancestral Connections: Art and Aboriginal Systems of Knowledge.* Chicago: University of Chicago Press.

———, ed. 1989. *Animals into Art.* Vol. 7. London: Unwin Hyman.

Munn, N. D. 1973. *Walbiri Iconography: Graphic Representation and Cultural Symbolism in a Central Australian Society.* Symbol, Myth, and Ritual Series. Ithaca: Cornell University Press.

Murkerjee, R. 1971. *The Social Function of Art.* Westport, Conn.: Greenwood Press.

Myerhoff, B. G. 1974. *Peyote Hunt: The Sacred Journey of the Huichol Indians.* Ithaca: Cornell University Press.

Nance, R. 1992. *The Archaeology of La Calsada: A Rock-shelter in the Sierra Madre Oriental, Mexico.* Austin: University of Texas Press.

Naranjo, C. 1973. Psychological Aspects of the Yagé Experience in an Experimental Setting. In *Hallucinogens and Shamanism,* edited by M. J. Harner, pp. 176–90. New York: Oxford University Press.

Narby, J. 1998. *The Cosmic Serpent.* New York: Putnam.

Newberg, A., E. D'Aquili, and V. Rause. 2001. *Why God Won't Go Away.* New York: Ballantine Books.

Norwine, Jim. 1995. The Regional Climate of South Texas: Patterns and Trends. In *The Changing Climate of Texas,* edited by Jim Norwine, J. Giardino, G. R. North, and J. Valdes, pp. 138–55. College Station: GeoBooks, Texas A&M University.

Office of the State Climatologist. 1987. Climates of Texas Counties. Austin: Graduate School of Business, University of Texas.

Opler, M. E. 1937. The Influence of Aboriginal Pattern and White Contact on a Recently Introduced Ceremony, the Peyote Rite. *Journal of American Folklore* 49:143–66.

———. 1938. The Use of Peyote by the Carrizo and Lipan Apache Tribes. *American Anthropologist* 40(2):271–85.

———. 1945. A Mescalero Apache Account of the Peyote Ceremony. *El Palacio* 52(10):210–12.

Ortiz, A. 1972. Ritual Drama and the Pueblo World-View. In *New Perspectives on the Pueblos,* edited by A. Ortiz, pp. 135–61. Albuquerque: University of New Mexico Press.

Ortiz de Montellano, B. R. 1975. Empirical Aztec Medicine. *Science* 188(4185):215–20.

———. 1990. *Aztec Medicine, Health, and Nutrition.* New Brunswick: Rutgers University Press.

Oster, G. 1970. Phosphenes. *Scientific American* 222(2):82–87.

Painter, E. H. 1986. *With Good Heart: Yaqui Beliefs and Ceremonies in a Pascua Village.* Tucson: University of Arizona Press.

Parkington, J. 1989. Interpreting Paintings without a Commentary: Meaning and Motive, Content and Composition in the Rock Art of the Western Cape, South Africa. *Antiquity* 63:13–26.

Parsons, E. W. C. 1936. *Mitla, Town of the Souls, and Other Zapotec-Speaking Pueblos of Oaxaca, Mexico.* Chicago: University of Chicago Press.

———. 1974. *Pueblo Indian Religion.* 4 vols. 1939. Reprint, Chicago: Midway Reprint.

Pasztory, E. 1983. *Aztec Art.* New York: Harry Abrams.

Pennington, C. M. 1963. *The Tarahumara of Mexico: Their Environment and Material Culture.* Salt Lake City: University of Utah Press.

Raun, G. 1966. A Vertebrate Paleofauna of Amistad Reservoir. In *A Preliminary Study of the Paleoecology of the Amistad Reservoir Area,* assembled by D. A. Story and V. M. Bryant, pp. 209–20. Final Report of Research under the Auspices of the National Science Foundation.

Rautenstrauch, R. K., and P. R. Krausman. 1989. The Influence of Water Availability and Rainfall on Movements of Desert Mule Deer. *Journal of Mammalogy* 70(1):197–201.

Reese, R. L., J. N. Derr, M. Hyman, M. W. Rowe, and S. K. Davis. 1996. Ancient DNA from Texas Pictographs. In *Archaeological Chemistry V: Organic, Inorganic, and Biochemical Analysis,* edited by M. V. Orna. Advances in Chemistry Series. Washington, D.C.: American Chemical Society.

Reichel-Dolmatoff, G. 1978a. *Beyond the Milky Way: Hallucinatory Images of the Tukano Indians.* Los Angeles: UCLA Latin American Center.

———. 1978b. Drug-Induced Optical Sensations and their Relationship to Applied Art among Some Columbian Indians. In *Art in Society,* edited by G. M. Greenhalgh and V. Megaw. London: Duckworth.

Reko, B. P. 1945. *Mitobotánica Zapoteca.* Tacubaya, Mexico: M. Soc. Botánica de México.

Renfrew, C., and P. Bahn. 1991. *Archaeology: Theories, Methods, and Practice.* New York: Thames and Hudson.

Renfrew, C., and E. Zubrow, eds. 1994. *The Ancient Mind: Elements of Cognitive Archaeology.* Cambridge: Cambridge University Press.

Richards, W. 1971. The Fortification Illusions of Migraines. *Scientific American* 225:89–96.

Ruecking, F. 1954. Ceremonies of the Coahuiltecan Indians. *Texas Journal of Science* 6(3):330–39.

Russ, J., M. Hyman, H. Shafer, and M. Rowe. 1990. Radiocarbon Dating of Prehistoric Rock Paintings by Selective Oxidation of Organic Carbon. *Nature* 348:710–11.

Russell, F. 1975. *The Pima Indians.* Tucson: University of Arizona Press.

Safford, W. E. 1916. Narcotic Plants and Stimulants of the Ancient Americas. In *Annual Report of the Board of Regents of the Smithsonian Institution,* pp. 387–424. Washington, D.C.: Government Printing Office.

Sahagún, Bernardino de. 1963. *Earthly Things.* Bk. 11, *Florentine Codex: General History of the Things of New Spain.* [1590?]. Translated by A. J. O. Anderson and C. E. Dibble. Santa Fe: School of American Research.

————. 1963. *The Origin of the Gods.* Bk. 3, *Florentine Codex: General History of the Things of New Spain.* [1590?]. Translated by A. J. O. Anderson and C. E. Dibble. Santa Fe: School of American Research.

————. 1920. Daturas of the Old World and New: An Account of their Narcotic Properties and Their Use in Oracular and Initiatory Ceremonies. In *Annual Report of the Board of Regents of the Smithsonian Institution,* pp. 537–67. Washington, D.C.: Government Printing Office.

Saunders, J. W. 1986. The Economy of Hinds Cave. Ph.D. dissertation, Southern Methodist University, Dallas.

Sayles, E. B. 1935. *An Archaeological Survey of Texas.* Medallion Papers XVII. Globe, Ariz.: Gila Pueblo.

Schaafsma, P. 1980. *Indian Rock Art of the Southwest.* Albuquerque: University of New Mexico Press.

Schaefer, S. B., and P. T. Furst, eds. 1996. *People of the Peyote: Huichol Indian History, Religion, and Survival.* Albuquerque: University of New Mexico Press.

Schele, L., and D. Freidel. 1990. *A Forest of Kings: The Untold Story of the Ancient Maya.* New York: William Morrow.

Schele, L., and M. Miller. 1986. *Blood of Kings: Dynasty and Ritual in Maya Art.* Fort Worth: Kimbell Art Museum.

Schleiffer, H. 1973. *Sacred Narcotic Plants of the New World Indians: An Anthology of Texts from the Sixteenth Century to Date.* New York: Hafner Press.

Schmidt, R. H. 1986. Chihuahuan Climate. In *Invited Papers from the Second Symposium on Resources of the Chihuahuan Desert Region, U.S. and Mexico,* edited by J. C. Barlow, A. M. Powell, and B. N. Timmermann. Alpine, Tex.: CDRI.

————. 1995. The Climate of Greater Trans-Pecos Texas. In *The Changing Climate of Texas,* edited by Jim Norwine, J. Giardino, G. R. North, and J. Valdes, pp. 138–55. College Station: GeoBooks, Texas A&M University.

Schroeder, A. H., and D. S. Matson. 1965. *A Colony on the Move: Gaspar Castaño de Sosa's Journal, 1590–1591.* Santa Fe: School of American Research.

Schultes, R. E. 1937. Peyote and Plants Used in Peyote Ceremonies. *Harvard Museum Leaflets* 4:129–52.

————. 1938. The Appeal of Peyote (*Lophophora Williamsii*) as a Medicine. *American Anthropologist* 40:698–715.

————. 1969. Hallucinogens of Plant Origin. *Science* 163(3862):245–54.

————. 1972. An Overview of Hallucinogens in the Western Hemisphere. In *Flesh of the Gods,* edited by P. T. Furst, pp. 3–54. New York: Praeger.

Shafer, H. J. 1975. Clay Figurines from the Lower Pecos River Region, Texas. *American Antiquity* 40(2):148–58.

————. 1980. Functional Interpretations of Lower Pecos Archaic Art. In *Papers on the Prehistory of Northeastern Mexico and Adjacent Texas,* edited by J. F. Epstein, T. R. Hester, and C. Graves, pp. 109–17. San Antonio: Center for Archaeological Research.

————. 1981. The Adaptive Technology of the Prehistoric Inhabitants of Southwest Texas. *Plains Anthropologist* 26(92):129–38.

————. 1986. *Ancient Texans: Rock Art and Lifeways along the Lower Pecos.* Austin: Texas Monthly Press.

————. 1988. The Prehistoric Legacy of the Lower Pecos Region of Texas. *Bulletin of the Texas Archaeological Society* 59:23–52.

Shafer H. J., and V. M. Bryant, Jr. 1977. *Archaeological and Botanical Studies at Hinds Cave, Val Verde County, Texas.* Texas A&M University. Report submitted to the National Science Foundation by the Department of Anthropology.

Sherratt, A. 1995. *Consuming Habits: Drugs in History and Anthropology.* London: Routledge.

Shonle, R. 1925. Peyote: The Giver of Visions. *American Anthropologist* 27:53–75.

Siegel, R. K. 1977. Hallucinations. *Scientific American* 237(4):132–41.

————. 1984. The Natural History of Hallucinogens. In *Hallucinogens: Neurochemical, Behavioral, and Clinical Perspectives,* edited by B. L. Jacobs, pp. 1–18. New York: Raven Press.

————. 1992. *Fire in the Brain: Clinical Tales of Hallucination.* New York: Dutton.

Siegel, R. K., and M. E. Jarvik. 1975. Drug-Induced Hallucinations in Animals and Man. In *Hallucinations: Behavior, Experience, and Theory,* edited by R. K. Siegel and L. J. West, pp. 81–161. New York: John Wiley and Sons.

Slotkin, J. S. 1951. Eighteenth-Century Documentation on Peyotism North of the Rio Grande. *American Anthropologist* 53:420–27.

————. 1955. Peyotism, 1521–1891. *American Anthropologist* 57:202–30.

Sobolik, K. D. 1991. *Paleonutrition of the Lower Pecos Region of the Chihuahuan Desert.* Ph.D. diss., Texas A&M University, College Station.

————. 1996. Nutritional Constraints and Mobility Patterns of Hunter-Gatherers in the Northern Chihuahuan Desert. In *Case Studies in Environmental Archeology,* edited by E. J. Reitz, L. A. Newsom, and S. J. Scudder, pp. 195–214. New York: Plenum Press.

Solomon, A. 1997. The Myth of Ritual Origins? Ethnography, Mythology, and Interpretation of San Rock Art. *South African Archaeological Bulletin* 52:3–13.

Spicer, E. H. 1940. *Pascua: A Yaqui Village in Arizona.* Chicago: University of Chicago Press.

Staniszewski, M. 1995. *Believing Is Seeing: Creating the Culture of Art.* New York: Penguin Books.

Stevenson, M. C. 1904. *The Zuni Indians: Their Mythology, Esoteric Fraternities, and Ceremonies.* Bureau of American Ethnology. Twenty-third Annual Report. Washington, D.C.: Government Printing Office.

———. 1915. *The Ethnobotany of the Zuni Indians.* Bureau of American Ethnology. Thirtieth Annual Report. Washington, D.C.: Government Printing Office.

Stewart, O. C. 1974. Origins of the Peyote Religion in the United States. *Plains Anthropologist* 19(65):211–23.

———. 1980. Peyotism and Mescalism. *Plains Anthropologist* 25(90):297–308.

———. 1987. *Peyote Religion.* Norman: University of Oklahoma Press.

Strong, W. D. 1929. Aboriginal Society in Southern California. *California University Publications in American Archaeology and Ethnology* 26:1–358.

Taçon, P. S. C. 1989. Art and the Essence of Being: Symbolic and Economic Aspects of Fish among the Peoples of Western Arnhem Land, Australia. In *Animals into Art,* edited by H. Morphy, pp. 236–50. London: Unwin Hyman.

Taylor, H. C. 1948. An Archaeological Reconnaissance of Northern Coahuilla. *Bulletin of the Texas Archaeological and Paleontological Society* 19:74–87.

———. 1949a. The Archaeology of the Area about the Mouth of the Pecos. Master's thesis, University of Texas.

———. 1949b. A Tentative Cultural Sequence for the Area about the Mouth of the Pecos. *Bulletin of the Texas Archaeological and Paleontological Society* 20:73–88.

Taylor, W. W. 1988. *Contributions to Coahuila Archaeology: With an Introduction to the Coahuila Project.* Center for Archaeological Investigations, Research Paper No. 52. Southern Illinois University, Carbondale.

Thoms, A. 1992. Late Pleistocene and Early Holocene Regional Land Use Patterns: A Perspective from the Preliminary Results of Archeological Studies at the Richard Beene Sties, 41BX831, Lower Medina River, South Texas. In *Guidebook, 10th Annual Meeting, South-Central Friends of the Pleistocene: Late Cenozoic Alluvial Stratigraphy and Prehistory of the Inner Gulf Coastal Plain, South-Central Texas.* Quaternary Research Center Series 4 (draft). Lubbock Lake Landmark, Texas Tech University, Lubbock.

Tooker, E., ed. 1979. *Native American Spirituality of the Eastern Woodlands.* Mahwah, N.J.: Paulist Press.

Troike, R. C. 1962. The Origins of Plains Mescalism. *American Anthropologist* 64:946–63.

Turner, E. S., and T. R. Hester. 1999. *A Field Guide to Stone Artifacts of Texas Indians.* Houston: Gulf Publishing.

Turner, V. 1967. *The Forest of Symbols.* Ithaca: Cornell University Press.

Turpin, S. A. 1984. The Red Linear Style Pictographs of the Lower Pecos River Region, Texas. *Plains Anthropologist* 29(105):181–98.

———. 1986. Toward a Definition of a Pictograph Style: The Lower Pecos Bold Line Geometrics. *Plains Anthropologist* 31(112):153–61.

———. 1990. Rock Art and Its Contribution to Hunter Gatherer Archaeology: A Case Study from the Lower Pecos River Region of Southwest Texas and Northern Mexico. *Journal of Field Archaeology* 17(3):263–81.

———. 1991. Sin Nombre and El Fortin: Pecos River Style Pictographs in Northern Mexico. *Bulletin of the Texas Archaeological Society* 60:267–78.

———. 1992. More Sacred Holes in the Ritual Landscape of the Lower Pecos River Region. *Plains Anthropologist* 37(140):275–78.

———. 1993. Hunting Camps and Hunting Magic: Petroglyphs of El Dorado Divide, West Texas. *North American Archaeologist* 13(4):295–316.

———. 1994. The Were-Cougar Theme in Pecos River Style Art and Its Implications for Traditional Archaeology. In *New Light on Old Art: Recent Advances in Hunter-Gatherer Rock Art Research,* edited by D. S. Whitley and L. L. Loendorf. Monograph 36. Los Angeles: Institute of Archaeology, University of California.

———. 1995. The Lower Pecos River Region of Texas and Northern Mexico. *Bulletin of the Texas Archaeological Society* 66:541–60.

———, ed. 1988. Seminole Sink: Excavation of a Vertical Shaft Tomb in Val Verde County, Texas. Memoir 22. *Plains Anthropologist* 33(122), pt.2.

Turpin, S. A., M. Henneberg, and D. Riskind. 1986. Late Archaic Mortuary Practices in the Lower Pecos River Region, Texas. *Plains Anthropologist* 31:295–315.

Tyler, C. 1978. Some New Entoptic Phenomena. *Vision Research* 18:1633–39.

Tyler, H. A. 1964. *Pueblo Gods and Myths.* Norman: University of Oklahoma Press.

Tylor, E. B. 1970. *Religion in Primitive Culture.* Gloucester, Mass.: Peter Smith.

Underhill, R. 1952. Peyote. In *Proceedings of the 30th International Congress of Americanists,* pp. 143–48, London.

———. 1969. *Papago Indian Religion.* 1946. Reprint, New York: AMS Press.

Valadez, S. 1996. Wolf Power and Interspecies Communication in Huichol Shamanism. In *People of the Peyote,* edited by S. Schaefer and P. Furst, pp. 267–305. Albuquerque: University of New Mexico Press.

Verstegan, R. 1628. *A Restitution of Decayed Intelligence in Antiquities: Considering the Most Noble and Renowned English Nation.* John Bill, Printer of the Kings Most Excellent Majesty. London.

Vinnicombe, P. 1967. Rock Painting Analysis. *South African Archaeological Bulletin* 22:129–41.

———. 1972. Myth, Motive, and Selection in Southern African Rock Art. *Africa* 42:192–204.

———. 1976. *People of the Eland: Rock Paintings of the Drakensberg Bushmen as a Reflection of Their Life and Thought.* Pietermeritzburg: Natal University Press.

Vogel, S. M. 1997. *Baule: African Art, Western Eyes.* New Haven: Yale University Press.

Watermann, T. T. 1910. The Religious Practices of the Diegueño Indians. *California University Publications in American Archaeology and Ethnology* 8(6):271–358.

Waters, F. 1963. *Book of the Hopi.* Penguin Group, New York.

Wellman, K. 1979. *A Survey of North American Indian Rock Art.* Graz, Austria: Akademische Druck- u. Verlagsanstalt.

Whiting, W. H. C. 1938. Journal of William Henry Chase Whiting, 1849. In *Exploring Southwestern Trails, 1846–1854,* edited by R. P. Beiber and A. B. Bender, pp. 241–350. Southwest Historical Series 7. Glendale, Calif.: Arthur H. Clark.

Whitley, D. S. 1987. Sociorelgious Context and Rock Art in East-Central California. *Journal of Anthropological Archaeology* 6:159–88.

———. 1992a. Prehistory and Post-Positivist Science. In *Advances in Archaeological Method and Theory,* edited by M. B. Schiffer. Vol. 4. Tucson: University of Arizona Press.

———. 1992b. Shamanism and Rock Art in Far-Western North America. *Cambridge Archaeological Journal* 2(1):89–113.

———. 1994a. By the Hunter, for the Gatherer: Art, Social Relations, and Subsistence Change in the Prehistoric Great Basin. *World Archaeology* 25:356–73.

———. 1994b. Ethnography and Rock Art in the Far West: Some Archaeological Implications. In *New Light on Old Art: Recent Advances in Rock Art Research,* edited by D. S. Whitley and L. L. Loendorf. Monograph 36. Los Angeles: Institute of Archaeology, University of California.

———. 1998. Finding Rain in the Desert: Rock Art and Landscape in Far Western North America. In *The Archaeology of Rock Art,* edited by C. Chippindale and P. S. C. Taçon. Cambridge: Cambridge University Press.

———. 1999. Sally's Rockshelter and the Archaeology of the Vision Quest. *Cambridge Archaeological Journal* 9(2):221–47.

Wilbert, J. 1987. *Tobacco and Shamanism in South America.* New Haven: Yale University Press.

Williams-Dean, G. 1978. Ethnobotany and Cultural Ecology of Prehistoric Man in Southwest Texas. Ph.D. diss., Texas A&M University, College Station.

Winkleman, M. 1986. Magico-Religious Practitioner Types and Socioeconomic Conditions. *Behavior Science Research* 20:17–46.

———. 1992. *Shamans, Priests, and Witches: A Cross-Cultural Study of Magico-Religious Practitioners.* Anthropological Research Papers No. 44. Arizona State University, Tempe.

Winters, W. 1975. The Continuum of CNS Excitatory States and Hallucinosis. In *Hallucinations: Behavior, Experience, and Theory,* edited by R. K. Siegel and L. J. West, pp. 53–70. New York: John Wiley and Sons.

Wright, P. A. 1989. The Nature of the Shamanic State of Consciousness: A Review. *Journal of Psychoactive Drugs* 21(1):25–33.

Yarnell, R. A. 1959. Prehistoric Pueblo Use of Datura. *El Palacio* 66(5):176–78.

Zingg, R. M. 1977. *Report of the Mr. and Mrs. Henry Pfeiffer Expedition for Huichol Ethnography: The Huichols, Primitive Artists.* 1938. Reprint, Millwood, N.Y.: Kraus Reprint.

Index

otherworld: and altered states of consciousness, 56, 59–60; archaeology of, 63; Aztec, 50, 51; Hopi, 54; Huichol, 52, 53; portals to, 49–55; shamanic journey to, 49–50; Yaqui, 53–54

otherworld journey motif, 45, 108; and cognitive neuroscience, 56–61; cosmology, graphic representation of, 65; at Cedar Springs, 48, 49; elements of, 45, 108; function of, 64–66, 112, 113; identified in ethnography, 50–54; at Mystic Shelter, 47, 48; at Panther Cave, 37, 47; at Rattlesnake Canyon, 33, 45, 46; at White Shaman, 46, 47

Otomi, and peyote, 73

painted pebbles, 15

Paiute, and datura use, 94

Panther Cave, 4, 31, 42; datura shamanism motif, 90; description of rock art panel, 35–36; location of, 35; otherworld journey motif, 37, 47; peyotism motif, 68, 69; plate 3

Papago (Tohono O'odham): coyote, 96; and peyote, 80–81; and datura use, 96

parietal lobe, 56

Pecos River, 9, 13, 31, 34, 73

Pecos River style: age, 19, 20; described, 16, 19, 20

peyote: alkaloids, 72, 111; as antidote for datura poisoning, 102; as antiwitch medicine, 102; in archaeological deposits, 72, 83, 113; birth of from deer antlers, 75; botany of, 70–73; geographic distribution of, 70, 71; as medicine, 73, 111; physiological effects of 72, 82, 111; and rainfall, 82, 83; relationship with deer, 70, 81–83, 100, 102–104, 107; —, Axacee, 81; Huichol, 74, 75, 76, 77, 78–79, 82, 83, 100, 102, 103; —, Native American Church, 81; —, Papago (Tohono O'odham), 80–81; —, Tamaulipecan, 81; —, Tarahumara, 81; —, Zapo-

tec, 80; as sacrament, 73, 113 visionary imagery associated with, 59, 72

peyote/deer/rain relationship, 81; ecological explanation for, 82–83; in Huichol ethnography, 74, 79; and neurophysiology of peyote intoxication, 82

peyotism: Huichol, 74–81; motif in lower Pecos rock art, 70, 109; —, ecological relationships communicated through, 83, 107, 111; origins of, 73–74, 83, 113; pictographic evidence of, 76–81, 113; tribes associated with, 73–74, 80–81, 83, 113

phosphenes, 57

photo reference form, 28, 117

pictographic elements: defined, 26, 27; geographic distribution of, 44; method for documentation and analysis of, 28, 30, patterned distribution of, 42, 44; referents for, 31

pictographic motif. See motif

Pima (Akmiel O'odham): and datura, 96; and peyote use, 73

politics, and rock art, 104

polysemy, 63, 64

portals. See axis mundi

predators: in the pictographs; 99–102; as animal counterparts for solanaceous plants, 99

Pressa Canyon, 79, 80, 100, 101, 102

psychotropic plants: and altered states of consciousness, 111; and rock art 67. See also datura; peyote

prickly pear, 11, 15, 17

rabbit-eared anthropomorphs: geographic distribution of, 31, 32, 33, 36, 42, 44, 112

radiocarbon ages, 13; of art, 19, 20; of peyote, 83

rain/deer/peyote relationship, 70, 74, 79, 82, 83, 107, 111

rainfall: annual average in lower Pecos, 10; and deer, 82

Rattlesnake Canyon, 4, 31, 42; datura shamanism motif, 91; otherworld journey motif, 45, 46; description of rock

art panel, 31–34; location of, 31; plate 1

Red Linear style: age, 20; and datura, 100, 101, 102; described, 20, 21; and peyotism, 79, 80

Red Monochrome style: age, 19, 20; described, 17, 19, 21; and peyotism, 79, 81, 100

Reichel-Dolmatoff, Gerardo, 57–58, 59

research design, 25–27

Rio Grande, 9, 11, 13, 31, 34, 73, 83

rock art: and adaptation, 4–8; as archaeological feature, 25; and artists as active agents; 5, 7, 104–105, 112, 114; explaining, 106–107; formulating hypotheses regarding, 27; function of, 64–66, 83, 104–105, 106–114; history of research in lower Pecos, 21, 22, 23; and ideology, 113; as indirect instruction, 7, 64, 65, 83, 107; and medical botany, 111; method for analysis, 27–31, 45, 106–107; panel defined, 26; politics, 104; recording and data collection, 27–31; reporting forms, 28–29, 116–123; and social relations, 65–66, 83, 112, 114; styles, 14; —, Bold Line Geometric, 23; Historic, 20, 21, 22; Pecos River, 16, 19, 20; —, Red Linear, 20, 21; Red Monochrome, 17, 19, 20, 21; and subsistence, 83, 107; as technology, 107, 111; and territoriality, 112

Rowe, Marvin, 24

sacred portal. See axis mundi

San, 64–65, 104–105

Seminole Canyon, 31, 35, 42, 78

Seminole Sink, 15, 63

serpent: and altered states of consciousness, 58, 59, 60; ethnographic motif containing, 49; —, in Aztec cosmology, 51; in Hopi cosmology, 54; —, in Huichol cosmology, 52; in Yaqui cosmology, 53–54; hallucinations of, 59; horned, 38, 42; identified in recurring

pictographic motif, 55, 59, 60, 63–64, 108
Shafer, Harry J., 23
shamanic ideologies: Aztec, 50; Hopi, 54; Huichol, 52; Yaqui, 53–54
shamanic journey: and altered states of consciousness, 49–50; and biology of trance, 56; and cognitivie neuroscience, 59–61; in ethnography, 49–54; hypothesis developed for rock art motif, 45, 56, *108;* and lower Pecos burial practices, 63; of neophytes (initiates), 65–66; psychotropic plants used in, 67, 70, 94; visionary experience, 65, 66. *See also* otherworld journey motif
shamans and shamanism: as artists, 61, 66, 83, 104, 105, 112; datura shamanism, 90–105, *110, 113;* defined, 49, 107; in ethnography, 49–54; function of, 49–50, 65, 66; key features of, 49–50; in lower Pecos rock art, 55, 54, 61, 62, 63, 64; as religious configuration, 107; tobacco shamanism, 99; wolf shamanism, 97
Shumla Caves, 83
single pole ladder: as anthropomorphs, 38; associated with antlered anthropomorphs, *40, 41, 78, 79;* associated with deer, 36, 38, 39, *40, 41, 78, 79, 80*
sinkholes: as portal to the otherworld, 63; burials in, 15, 63

site form, 28, 116
skeletonization: and shamanism, 50, 55; in Huichol art, 52, 53. *See also* centrastyled anthropomorphs
snakes. *See* serpents
Sophora secundiflora. See mescal beans
sorcery, 96, 98, 102
sotol, 15, 16, 18
subsistence, and rock art, 83, 107

Tamaulipeco, and peyote use, 73, 81
Tarahumara: and peyote use, 73, 81, 102; and datura, 94, 102
Tarascan, and peyote use, 73
Teochichimeca, 74
Tepecano, and peyote use, 73
Tepehuan, and peyote use, 73
therianthropes (human-animal): and altered states, 60–61; defined, 29, 31
Tlascalan, and peyote, 73
tobacco shamanism, 99
Tonkawa, and peyote, 73
Tukano, visionary art, 59
tunnels, 59, 60
Turpin, Solveig, 23, 63, 99

underworld. *See* otherworld
universe, tiered, 49, 54, 63, 113. *See also* otherworld

visionary art, importance of, 64–66

werewolves, 98
White Shaman, 4, 31, *42;* datura shamanism, 91, 104; description of rock art panel, 34–35; and Huichol peyote pilgrimage, 76–78; location of, 34;

otherworld journey motif, 46, *47;* peyotism motif, 67, *68, 69,* 76–78, *109,* 113; *plate 2*
Wilbert, Johannes, 99
witchcraft: and coyote, 96, 97, 98, 99; and datura, 96, 97, and solanaceous hallucinogens, 97–99
Witte Memorial Museum, 21, 23
wolf shamanism, 97

Yaqui: and caves, 53, 54; cosmology, 53; coyote, 96; serpents as portals to the otherworld, 53; —, as provider of ritual, 54; animal spirit helpers, 54; and peyote use, 73; shamanic ideology, 53–54; witches, 96
Yokut, and datura use, 94
yucca, 11, 12, 15, 16, 18; as emulsifier in paint, 24
Yuman, and datura use, 94

Zacateco, and peyote use, 73
Zapotec: datura, 96, 97; and peyote, 80; witches, 97
Zopilote Cave, 84
zoomorph: defined, 28; identified during feature analysis, *42;* —, at Cedar Springs, 39; —, at Mystic Shelter, 37–38; —, at Panther Cave, 36; —, at Rattlesnake Canyon, 33; at White Shaman, 34–35
Zuni: coyote, 96; and datura, 94, 96, 97; witchcraft, 96; squash blossom, 94

ISBN 1-58544-259-3